the me I **want** to be

student edition

the me I **want** to be

student edition

john ortberg

with scott rubin

ZONDERVAN

The Me I Want to Be, Student Edition

This title is also available as a Zondervan ebook. Visit www.zondervan.com/ebooks.

Requests for information should be addressed to:

Zondervan, *3900 Sparks Drive SE, Grand Rapids, Michigan 49546*

This edition: ISBN 978-0-310-74863-2

Library of Congress Cataloging-in-Publication Data

Ortberg, John.
The me I want to be : becoming God's best version of you / John Ortberg with Scott Rubin. — Teen ed.
p. cm.
Includes bibliographical references.
ISBN 978-0-310-67112-1 (softcover)
1. Christian teenagers — Religious life. I. Rubin, Scott. II. Title.
BV4531.3.O77 2010
248.8'3 — dc22 2010024888

Other translations used are the *New International Version* (NIV), the *New American Standard Bible* (NASB), the King James Version (KJV), the *New Revised Standard Version* (NRSV), the *New Living Translation* (NLT), the *Living Bible* (TLB), and *The Message* (MSG).

Any Internet addresses (websites, blogs, etc.) and telephone numbers in this book are offered as a resource. They are not intended in any way to be or imply an endorsement by Zondervan, nor does Zondervan vouch for the content of these sites and numbers for the life of this book.

Cover and interior design: Lindsay Lang Sherbondy with Heartland Community Church
Interior design management: Ben Fetterley

First printing 2010 / Printed in the United States of America
HB 01.12.2018

contents

PART ONE

finding my identity

»

Chapter 1

Learn Why God Made You

Do you ever ask the question, *What am I doing here?*

Do you ever wonder, out of all the people walking around on this planet, *Why did God make* me?

One week it was all the rage on Facebook to replace your profile picture with the photo of a celebrity who could be your double or look-alike. Some call it your *doppelgänger*, which means "double-goer." I noticed a lot of people chose extremely attractive celebrities for their doppelgängers and claimed that people say they look "just like them." I wondered if some of those people might need contact lenses.

There are around seven billion people living on planet Earth. 7,000,000,000. That's a lot of people. And there are no "repeats." No doubles. No "extras." Absolutely every individual on this globe is a person who God meant to be here.

So, if God really wants us here, have you ever considered this next question?

What do you really want?

What *I* really want is to be fully alive inside. What *I* really want is the freedom to live in love and excitement and wonder and passion. What *I* want is to Really Live.

But there are a lot of other things people get preoccupied with, aren't there? When you're in school, you can be absorbed with getting good grades or getting cute people to like you. As the years go by, lots of people become preoccupied with jobs and families and hobbies. But I believe God made us for much more than just being preoccupied with things ... even good things.

I want to Really Live more than I want anything else. Not because I think I'm supposed to, and not because it says somewhere that I should—I want it.

There is a me I want to be.

Life is not about any particular achievement or experience. The most important mission of your life is not what you do but who you become.

There is a me you want to be, too.

Ironically, just as no one becomes happy if the main goal is happiness, becoming this person will never happen to you or to me if our primary focus is on us. God made you to Really Live—but Really Living never happens by looking out for number one. It's tied to a grander and better vision. The world badly needs human beings who are Really Living, and you and I are called to bring God's wisdom and glory to the world through Really Living.

The truth is, those who Really Live always bring blessings to others—and they can do so in the most unexpected and humble circumstances.

» What Does It Mean to "Really Live" This Life?

There are two school bus drivers. Both drivers are safe and run their routes on time, but that's where the similarities seem to end.

The first bus driver picks up students, but he never really looks them in the eye. He doesn't acknowledge them when they hop on the bus in the morning, or when they drag themselves back on the bus after a long day at school. He's not super-mean, but he's crabby when students laugh too loud. He's focused on getting them where they need to go, but he has a brain full of personal concerns and worries that he's keeping track of, too. He's never learned the names of any of the students on his route; maybe because of that, none of the kids know his name, either.

The other bus driver's name is Phil. Students are pretty tired in the morning, but just a few weeks into the school year, Phil greeted them all by name as they boarded the bus. Often he'll notice if they're carrying projects for one of their classes and ask if they need extra room for them. He lets the kids vote on which radio station plays during the ride, and on Fridays he turns up the volume a little louder. Students like telling jokes to Phil, and he'll often have one to tell them in return. And if somebody's running late, that student can count on Phil to wait an extra minute as the student runs down the street to catch the bus. Phil has a brain full of personal concerns and worries, too; but while he's on that bus route, he's more than just a driver—he's the leader of the bus. Phil is moving toward the best version of himself.

Are you sometimes like that first bus driver—the one who can't get beyond himself to show love toward others? We all are, in different ways and at different times. But even when you're acting like the first bus driver, sometimes you do something that surprises you—and you catch a glimpse of the person you were made to be. You say something encouraging in a classroom. At school you talk to the kid who most people completely ignore. You're patient with an irritating little brother. You lose yourself in a song. You show compassion. You stand up to a bully. You willingly make a gift that costs you something. You forgive someone who hurt you. You say something you'd normally never say, or you stop yourself from saying something you'd normally blurt out.

As you do these things, you get a glimpse of why God made you. Only God knows your full potential, and God's guiding you toward that best version of yourself all the time. God has lots of tools and is never in a hurry. This waiting can be frustrating; but even in your frustration, God is at work to produce patience in you. God never gets discouraged by how long it takes, and God's thrilled every time you grow. Only God can see the "best version of you," and God is more concerned with your reaching your full potential than you are.

"For we are God's handiwork, created in Christ Jesus to do good works, which God prepared in advance for us to do."

You are not *your* handiwork; your life is not *your* project. Your life is *God's* project. God thought you up, and God knows what you were intended to be. Did anyone ever ask you, "What do you want to *be* when you grow up?" Did you ever feel like maybe you should have an answer—even when you don't have one? Well, God has an answer. God wants you to be the best possible version of *you!* God has many good works for you to do, but God's good work isn't like homework or chores. God's good work points you back to your true self.

Your "spiritual life" isn't just about stuff like going to church, reading your Bible, and praying a prayer; it's about receiving power from the Spirit of God to become the person God had in mind when God thought you up.

» Where Growth Leads

God made you to Really Live—to get strength from outside yourself, create energy within yourself, and give blessing beyond yourself. Really Living is God's gift and plan. And when you Really Live, you're synched up with God, other people, creation, and yourself. Really Living isn't measured by outward signs such as chasing after honors or awards or getting more possessions or trying to be really attractive. It means becoming the person *God* had in mind when God created you.

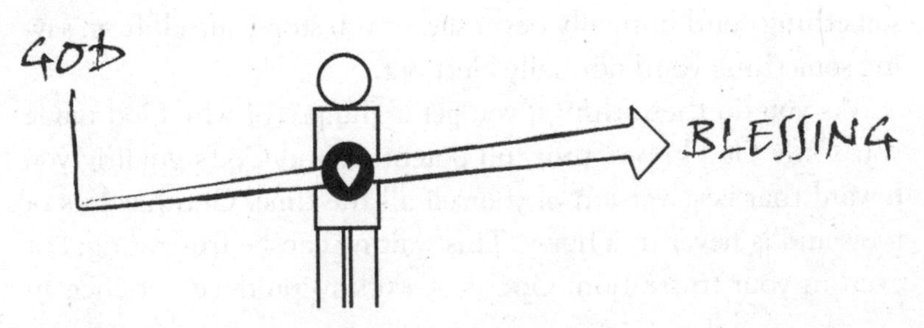

Really Living means moving toward God's best version of you.

> The righteous will flourish like a palm tree ... they will flourish in the courts of our God. (Psalm 92:12–13)

As God helps you grow, you'll change; but you'll always be *you*. An acorn can grow into an oak tree, but it *can't* become a rosebush. It can be a healthy oak, or it can be an undergrown oak—but it won't be a shrub. It can't be! In the same way, you'll always be you—either a growing, healthy you or a weak version of you. God didn't create you to be anybody else. God prewired your personality. God chose your natural gifts and talents. God made you to feel certain passions and desires. God planned your body and mind. Your uniqueness is God-designed.

Some people believe that if they want to grow spiritually, they have to become different people. But God doesn't want you to be someone else. God wants you to be you ... even though God may redirect you. Before Paul met Jesus, he was a brilliant, passionate zealot who assaulted others. Afterward, he was a brilliant, passionate zealot who sacrificed himself for others.

Some friends of ours have a daughter named Shauna who, at age four, was a classic strong-willed child. For example, she kept trying to take off on her tricycle, ready to ride far beyond where her mother was comfortable. Shauna's mom couldn't hold her back, and she finally said, "Look, Shauna, there's a tree right here, and there's a driveway right there. You can ride your tricycle on the sidewalk between the driveway and the tree, but you can't go past that—or you're going to get a spanking. I have to be inside; I've got stuff to do. But I'm going to be watching you."

Shauna backed up to her mom, pointed to her spanking zone, and said, "Well, you might as well spank me now because I got places to go."

Would it surprise you to learn that when Shauna grew up, she had amazing leadership abilities and a huge sense of determination? She'll always have them.

God doesn't make anything and then decide to throw it away. God creates and then, if there's a problem, God rescues. The guy who wrote Psalm 100 says, "Know that the LORD Himself is God; it is He who has made us, and not we ourselves."

Here's the good news: When you flourish—when you Really Live—you become more you. You become more that person God had in mind when God thought you up. You don't just become holier. You become you-ier. You'll change; God wants you to become a "new creation." But "new" doesn't mean completely different; instead, it's like an old piece of furniture that gets restored to its intended beauty.

I used to have a chair that my grandfather helped build 70 years ago. I loved it, but its arms were broken, the wood was chipped, and the cushioning was worn through. I finally gave up on it and sold it for 50 cents at a garage sale. The person who bought it knew about restoration; and a few months later, I received a picture of it—repaired and refinished. I wish this were one of those stories where the restorer surprises the clueless owner by giving back the now-glorious chair. But all I have is this attractive picture. Still, I keep the picture taped inside my desk drawer to remind me that "if anyone is in Christ, the new creation has come: The old has gone, the new is here!"

God doesn't make anything and then decide to throw it away.

God wants to redeem you, not exchange you. So if you're a quiet, reflective person who's hoping God will change you into an extrovert, have fun waiting—it'll be a long wait. Or if you're a big-time extrovert who's hoping God will turn you into a quieter individual—again, have fun waiting. It's never going to happen.

It's humbling to know that I cannot be anything I want. I don't get to create myself. I accept myself as God's gift to me and accept becoming that person as God's mission for me. But inside your soul there's a battle between a self that Really Lives—the person you were created to be—and a decaying self. This book is all about that battle as it moves from deep inside you to a world waiting for God's rescue.

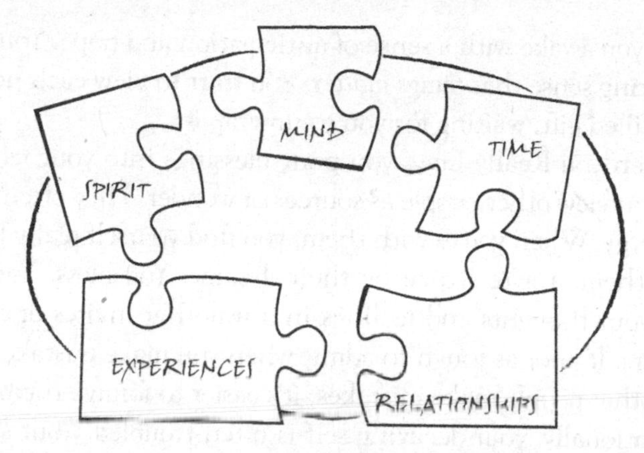

The journey starts with your *spirit,* which becomes empowered by God's Spirit. You know that feeling when you're getting ideas or energy from a source beyond yourself? In other words, you're being *in-spired*—a Spirit-word that literally means something has been breathed into you. So this sense of Really Living—being connected with the Spirit of God—is available all the time! And when your spirit Really Lives, you're most fully alive. You have a purpose for living. You're pulled toward goodness and away from sin.

Then there's your *mind.* The mental life of your Really-Living self is marked by joy and peace. You're curious and love to learn. You do this in your own unique way, whether through reading or talking with people or listening or building or leading. You ask questions. You're not easily bored. When negative emotions come up, you take them as reminders to take some action.

Your decaying self, on the other hand, feels uneasy and restless inside. You find yourself drawn to bad habits—watching way too much TV or isolating yourself or doing things you know are destructive—because they're attempts to make pain go away. In your decaying self, thoughts drift toward fear or anger. Learning doesn't feel worth the effort. You think a lot of selfish thoughts—and not much about other people.

Along with your spirit and mind, when you Really Live your *time* starts to be transformed as well. You have confidence that whatever life throws at you won't overthrow you. When the day dawns, you awake with a sense of anticipation and hope. You have an exciting sense that *things matter.* You start to view each hour as a God-filled gift, waiting for you to unwrap it.

When you Really Live, you pour blessings into your *relationships*. You view other people as sources of wonder. They often bring you energy. When you're with them, you find yourself really listening to them. You're struck by their dreams. You bless. You talk about your thoughts and feelings in a way that invites openness in others. It's not as tough to admit when you make mistakes; and when other people make mistakes, it's easier to forgive them.

Relationally, your decaying self is often troubled. Your speech is out of control—sometimes you're super-sarcastic, or you gossip, or you say things that aren't even true. You isolate. You dominate. You attack. You withdraw.

But as God grows you, God wants to use you in his plan to redeem the world, and you find God changing your *experiences*. Your Really-Living self wants to contribute. You have a sense that your life really counts for something—that it really matters. You become tougher in the face of suffering. You get better. You grow.

What could you want more than to become the person God created you to be?

» The World God Wants to See

Here are some great secrets you can find in the Bible:

Your desire to become all you were meant to be is just a tiny echo of God's desire to begin that new creation.

The more concerned you are about your own satisfaction, the less satisfied you'll be.

When your life is all about you, it's as small as a grain of wheat; when your life is given to God, however, it's as if that grain is planted in rich soil, growing into part of a much bigger project.

I get hung up on so many things in life, worrying about what I'll never do or achieve or have. But I don't want to miss out on what God has for me! I want to love my family and give life to my friends. I want to do the stuff God made me to do. I want to love God and the world God made.

I want to do my part to Really Live because my spiritual growth isn't measured by following rules; "the me God made me to be" is measured by how much I love. When we live in love, we Really Live. And the time to love is now. Not when you're older. Not when you "get your act together." That's the whole ballgame.

In many ways this life is a kind of school for the next life—a kind of preparation for the me you were meant to be. Because that person will go into eternity. And what matters most isn't what you accomplish; it's who you become.

God's ready to help you become The Me You Want to Be.

Are *you* ready?

Chapter 2

The Me I Don't Want to Be

Henri Nouwen was a legendary priest and teacher who taught at highly respected universities like Harvard and Yale and Notre Dame. But Henri came to believe that those settings did not—for him—bring out the person God intended him to be. So this famous writer spent the last 10 years of his life caring for physically and mentally challenged people at a small community called L'Arche.

While he was there, Henri made friends with a resident named Trevor who had many mental and emotional challenges. One time when Trevor was sent to a hospital for evaluation, Henri called to arrange a visit. When the people who ran this hospital found out that the famous Henri Nouwen was coming, they asked if he'd meet with some doctors and other "important" people. He agreed, and when he arrived, there was a fabulous luncheon set up in a special place called the Golden Room—but Trevor wasn't there.

"Where is Trevor?" Henri asked.

"He cannot come to the lunch," they told him. "Patients and staff are not allowed to have lunch together, and no patient has ever had lunch in the Golden Room."

"But the whole purpose of my visit was to have lunch with Trevor," Henri said. "If Trevor is not allowed to attend the lunch, then I will not attend either."

Somehow, they suddenly found a way for Trevor to attend the lunch.

The Golden Room was filled with adults who were really excited that the great Henri Nouwen was in their midst. Some tried to get up close to him. They thought of how great it would be to tell their friends, "I got to hang out with Henri Nouwen the other day . . ." Some pretended to have read books they hadn't read and to appear smarter than they really were. Others were upset that the rule about separating patients and staff had been broken.

Trevor didn't take notice of the fuss; he just sat next to Henri. And at one point when Henri was talking to the person on his other side, he didn't notice when Trevor stood up to speak to the crowd.

"A toast," Trevor said. "I will now offer a toast."

The room grew quiet. *What in the world is this guy going to do?*

Then Trevor began to sing.

> *If you're happy and you know it, raise your glass.*
> *If you're happy and you know it, raise your glass.*
> *If you're happy and you know it, if you're happy and you know it,*
> *If you're happy and you know it, raise your glass.*

At first people weren't sure how to respond, but Trevor was beaming. His face and voice told everyone how glad and proud he was to be there with his friend Henri. Somehow Trevor, in his brokenness and joy, gave a gift no one else in the room could give. People started to sing — softly at first, but then with more enthusiasm — until doctors and priests and Ph.D.s were almost shouting, "If you're happy and you know it . . ."

And they did it all under the direction of Trevor.

No one was trying to show off anymore. No one worried about the rules. No one tried to separate the Ph.D.s from the ADDs. For a few moments, a room full of people moved toward the best version of themselves because a guy named Henri Nouwen made a choice to live among the challenged—and because a challenged guy named Trevor was living out the best version of himself.

We don't just drift into becoming the best version of ourselves. If I want to become the person I want to be, then I have to come to grips with the fake versions of me that try to force their way in—and prevent me from becoming the me I'm meant to be.

» The Me I Pretend to Be

God designed you to be you. When your life is over, God won't ask you why you weren't Moses or Peter or Mary or your English teacher or your mom or dad or your Uncle Louie. If you don't pursue the life we're talking about here, then God will ask why you weren't *you*. God designed us to *delight* in our actual lives.

You see, when I'm growing toward the me I *want* to be, I'm being freed from the me I *pretend* to be. I stop trying to convince people I'm important while secretly fearing that I'm not important.

But sometimes the me I pretend to be leaks out when I try to show how "important" I am. It happens to other people, too. A brand-new principal at a high school wanted to impress the first custodian who entered his new office, so the principal pretended to be on the phone with the superintendant of the school district. "Yes sir, Mr. Superintendant, you can count on me!" the principal said before banging down the receiver. Then he asked the custodian what he wanted. "I'm just here to connect your phone, sir."

Pretending to be someone we're not is hard work, which is why it's tiring to act like someone else or to be someplace where we feel as though we have to project a certain image. That's why we're usually drawn to people who are honest about who they are and we hunger to go places where we can just "be ourselves."

Isn't it a relief to know that we don't need to do that with God? We don't have to pretend to pray more than we really do, or to know more about the Bible than we really know, or to act more humble or more popular or smarter than we really are. No, we never have to pretend with God. Believe it or not, genuineness—even when it's brokenness—*thrills* God! Pretend spirituality most definitely annoys God.

And if I'm ever going to become the me I want to be, then I have to start by being honest about the me that I *am*.

» The Me I Think I *Should* Be

> Henri Nouwen wrote, "Spiritual greatness has nothing to do with being greater than others. It has everything to do with being as great as each of us can be."

Each one of us has a "me" that we think we *should* be, which is at odds with the me that God *made* each of us to be. Sometimes letting go of that self may be a relief. Sometimes it won't feel good at all.

Lots of us try on different images in school. We get the sense from others that there's a "right" person to be—the person we "should" be. But the truth is we need to let go of that should-be person and look deeply into who God really made us to be.

I grew up with a need to think of myself as a leader—as stronger, more popular, more confident than I really was. I ran for class president because grown-up leaders would always say, "When I was in high school, I was class president." I created catchy slogans and campaigned hard—but I always lost. To be honest, I was more introverted and less of a "class president type" than I wanted anyone to know.

Yet as I grew older, my need to be a leader kept me trying to be somebody I wasn't. It made me more defensive, pressured, unhappy, and inauthentic in ways I didn't even realize. To make matters worse, the person I married is one of those people who ran for school offices—and always won. She didn't even have a good slogan: "Don't be fancy, vote for Nancy." (No, I'm not making that up. She actually *won* with that.)

It wasn't until I was an adult that I finally said to God, "I give up my need to be a leader." Out of me came a volcano of emotion. I felt like all my dreams had died. All I knew was that holding on to my need to lead was wrecking my life. So I prayed, "I'll let it go. It's been my dream for so long that I don't know what's left. If I can't become this leader I thought I was supposed to be, I don't know what to do. But I'll try to do the best I can to let it go."

What I was really dying to was a false self, an illusion of misplaced pride, ego, and neediness—the me I thought I was *supposed* to be.

Should is an important word for spiritual growth. God's plan isn't for you to obey him because you *should*, even though you don't want to. God made you to *want* his plan for you!

» The Me Other People Want Me to Be

Everyone in your life wants you to change. Your teacher wants you to study more. Your coach wants you to get in better shape. Your parents want you to act with more courtesy. TV stations want you to watch more TV. Fast-food places want you to eat more burgers. Everybody has an agenda for you—the me other people want you to be.

If I spend my life trying to become *that* me, I'll never be free. Loving people means being willing to disappoint them sometimes. Jesus loved everyone, but that means at some point he disappointed everyone. Seeking to become the me other people want me to be is a hollow way to live. Nobody else can tell you exactly how to change because nobody but God knows.

Even you can't tell yourself how to change—because you didn't create you! To love someone is to desire and work toward that person becoming the best version of himself or herself. And the only one in the universe who can do this perfectly is God—the only one with no other agenda. God has no unmet needs that you need to help meet. And God *knows* what the best version of you looks like. God's thrilled by the idea of the best you, and God is already working on it. The apostle Paul wrote, "We know that in all things God works for the good of those who love him."

This means God is at work every moment to help you become God's best version of you.

» The Me I'm Afraid God Wants

A team of researchers called the Barna Group recently conducted a survey that found the number-one obstacle to spiritual growth is that most people believe spiritual maturity means trying hard to follow the rules in the Bible. No wonder survey respondents also said they're unmotivated to pursue spiritual growth! If we believe God's ultimate goal is to produce rule-followers, then spiritual growth will always be a chore or a duty instead of a desire of our hearts.

"Rule-keeping does not naturally evolve into living by faith," Paul wrote, "but only perpetuates itself in more and more rule-keeping." In other words, it only results in a desire-smothering, Bible-reading, emotion-controlling, self-righteous person who is not like *me*. I can't follow God if I don't trust that God really has my best interests at heart.

A friend of mine recently graduated from one of those military academies where they're very serious about the "clean your room" rule. Sometimes my friend got ink marks on the wall that wouldn't come off, so he chipped off the plaster instead. And while the inspectors busted people for ink marks, they figured missing chunks of plaster were construction problems. The "rules" ended up encouraging the slow demolition of the room.

Jesus did not say, "I have come that you might follow the rules." He said, "I have come that you might have life, and have it with abundance." When we stop looking at spiritual growth as moving toward God's best version of ourselves, we're scared by the question, *How's your spiritual life going?* A nagging sense of guilt makes us say, "Not too well. Not as good as I should be doing."

Way too often people use outer behaviors to measure their spiritual health. They judge their spiritual lives by how early they're getting up to read the Bible, or how long their quiet times are, or how often they go to church. (And those things can be helpful—there's nothing wrong with them.) But that's not what spiritual growth is about.

» The Me That Fails to Be

Oftentimes people have dreams for their lives when they're young, but over time they simply give up. A writer named Gordon MacKenzie tells of visiting children in first grade and asking them, "Who in this room is an artist?" Every hand shoots up. This decreases to half the class by third grade. And by the time the students are 12 years old, only a few hands go up. Anybody notice fewer artists in your classes as you've gotten older? How did that happen? Over time a lot of people find that becoming the me they were meant to be is too hard or takes too long. When we give up on our growth and life's purpose, we miss out!

But there's a person inside you waiting to come alive.

» The Me I'm Meant to Be

God wants you to grow! God created the original *idea* of growth. God invented it.

Really Living is never just about you; it's a "so that" kind of thing. In other words, God designed you to Really Live "so that" you could be part of God's mission on earth; or God wants you to Really Live "so that" people can be encouraged, gardens can be planted, music can be written, sick people can be helped, and schools can thrive. So when you fail to become the person God designed, all the rest of us miss out on the gift you were made to give!

Jesus once said that with God, all things are possible—and the great thing about life with God is that your next step is always possible. That step toward God is always waiting, no matter what you've done or how you've messed up your life. When Jesus was hanging on a cross with a thief hanging on a cross next to him,

have life

Jesus said, "I have come that they may have life, and have it to the full." We may have heard that without understanding what Jesus offers. When he says he's come that we "may have life," what *exactly* does he mean?

We might think that we know what life is, but life turns out to be surprisingly tricky to define. So we might start here: *Life is the inner power to make something happen.*

Throw a rock, and it soon stops moving. But put a seed in the ground, and something happens — it sends out a root, takes in nourishment, and grows up to be fruitful. To be spiritually alive means to receive power from God to have a positive impact on your world.

What are some ways God uses to give life and vitality to you? How can you build these into your life and schedule?

- Nature
- Spiritual friendships
- Music
- Solitude
- Serving
- Learning
- Leading
- Art
- Rest
- Competition
- Scripture
- Recreation
- Exercise
- Family
- Long talks
- Laughter
- Leading a cause
- Retreat
- Small group
- Other

Saint Irenaeus writes, "The glory of God is a human being fully alive; and to be alive consists in beholding God."

Jesus turned to him and said, "Today you will be with me in paradise."

You can always take a next step.

So I propose a toast: "Here's to Trevor. And to Henri. And to the me you want to be."

PART TWO

flowing with the spirit

Chapter 3
Discover the Flow

Really Living *is* possible.

I don't have to wait for stuff in my life to change in order to live the way I was meant to live. I just have to want it more than I want anything else. Most of the time, though, I let my mind get pulled in lots of different directions. Or I just let my mind go and think about nothing at all.

Or I worry. About school. Or about who I want to date (and how I could get him or her to date me). Or about a competition that's coming up or a project I need to complete. Or my parents. Somehow I believe that if I worry about all these things, they'll go better, and I'll be happy and free. (Yeah, right!)

The truth is, a life of freedom and joy is available right now—and there's no need to waste time worrying about it. All I have to do is remain connected to God. When my primary focus is being right here *with* God, everything else has a way of falling into place. (Sounds almost too simple, doesn't it? But it's true!) However, when my primary focus becomes anything else, my inner vitality suffers, and I become a lesser version of myself.

My wife is a longtime water skier. While we were on vacation one summer, she taught our family to water-ski. I'd water-skied only once or twice before, so it took several trips around the lake for me to feel any confidence at all. Then I decided I wanted to try using only one ski, but the boat couldn't generate enough power for me to stand up.

When I got back in the boat, I noticed a button labeled POWER TILT. I don't know much about boats or engines, but it seemed like a promising button. So we gave it a shot, and I heard a whirring sound, which I later learned was the propeller being driven much deeper under the water.

I got back behind the boat, balanced insecurely on one ski, and yelled to Nancy, "Hit it!"

The bow of the boat lifted out of the water at a 45-degree angle and blasted off like it was being shot from a cannon. Now standing up wasn't a problem—*survival* was a problem! I gestured wildly for the boat to slow down, but we hadn't set up any signals ahead of time. So my kids figured my frantic waving meant I wanted to go faster, and they revved the boat *full throttle*. I was bouncing through the air between landings like a rock skipping across a lake. And for some reason I didn't think of just letting go of the rope. I eventually did a major face-plant.

For six months I couldn't smile with the right side of my mouth.

But I did find out that I could water-ski—I just needed power.

In the same way, trying to become the person you were made to be through your own power is like trying to ski behind a rowboat.

We need a "power tilt" for the soul.

So where do we find it?

Jesus made shocking promises about his ability to transform human lives:

"'Let anyone who is thirsty come to me and drink. Whoever believes in me, as Scripture has said, rivers of living water will flow from within them.' By this he meant the Spirit, whom those who believed in him were later to receive."

The King James Bible states it this way: "Out of his belly shall flow rivers of living water." The belly is the deepest place inside you—the place where you get anxious or afraid, where you feel hollow or empty when you're disappointed. It's in that very deepest place that Jesus says he'll produce vitality.

This life isn't something we produce; it exists without our help. It comes from the Spirit of God. If we turn to any book in the New Testament, we see a picture of amazing life offered by Jesus through the Spirit.

"You will receive power when the Holy Spirit comes on you."

"Though you have not seen [Jesus], you love him . . . and are filled with an inexpressible and glorious joy."

"Take my yoke upon you and learn from me, for I am gentle and humble in heart, and you will find rest for your souls."

Would you say these verses describe you? Are you filled with glorious joy? Do others comment that you've pretty much aced the gentleness thing?

After people say yes to Jesus in their lives, there's usually a kind of spiritual honeymoon period. New Christians are filled with love for God, and they're drawn to the Bible. They want to tell other people about their faith. They love to worship. And some things change in their lives, too. Maybe foul language gets cleaned up. Maybe certain habits get overcome.

But after a little while, this sense of progress often stalls out. Instead of life flowing with rivers of living water, I yell at my family members. I worry too much about school or relationships. I get jealous. I lie to get out of trouble or to get what I want. I judge people easily and look down on them. My prayer life is on and off. I'm stuck in a gap.

God's plan is for you to become the best version of you, but right now there are two versions of you: The you God made you to be—and the you right now.

What do you do with the gap?

» Gap Management

Our problem is that we believe we have to close the gap through our own cleverness. Some believe that if they just try harder, they can close the gap between the me God made them to be and the me right now. They believe they're just not being heroic enough in their spiritual efforts: "I'll work harder. I'll try to be nicer to the people in my life. I'll pray more. I'll pay more attention at youth group."

You hear about someone who gets up early in the morning to pray, and you feel guilty because you think you don't pray enough. So you make up your mind to wake up early, too (even though you're not a "morning person"). Only, when you wake up early, you're dazed and groggy and grumpy, and no one wants to be around you. You think, *Well, this is exhausting and miserable. I sure don't like doing it—therefore, it must be God's will for my life.* You keep it up for several days or weeks or maybe even months—but not forever. Eventually you stop. Then you feel guilty. After enough guilt, you start doing something else.

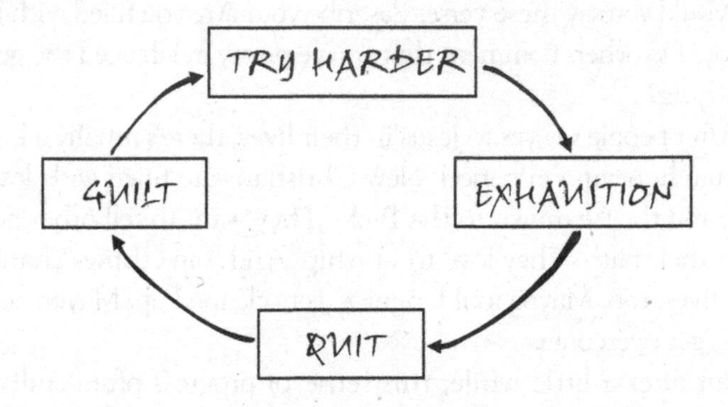

Sometimes we manage the gap by pretending. We learn to fake it. We speak as if we're walking closer to God than we really are, as though our sin bothers us more than it really does. We try to pray impressive prayers. Some people rush from one spiritual experience to another, continually rededicating their lives to God at camps or retreats or church services, hoping to recapture the emotions they felt when they first met God. And then they fall away again.

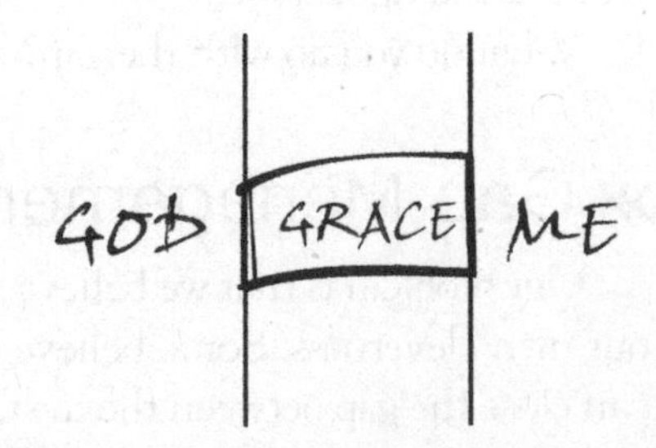

At the beginning of our life with God, we're aware of a gap between God and us—separation from God because of sin.

We soon come to understand that we can't bridge this gap by our efforts or good behavior. We can't earn God's love and forgiveness; salvation is given by the grace of God, accomplished through the power of God, offered through the Spirit of God. And so we commit our lives to God.

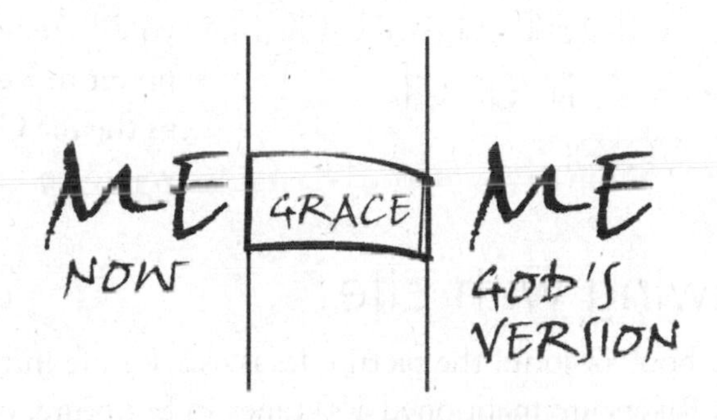

But there's still a gap.

Now the gap is between the me I am right now and the me I'm meant to be — "the now me" and "God's version of me." But here's the problem: A lot of us believe it's *our job* to bridge that gap. But we can't make that happen, either. This gap can be bridged only by grace. Improving yourself on your own makes as much sense as saving yourself on your own — you can't! God's plan isn't just for us to be *saved* by grace — it's for us to *live* by grace. God's plan is for my daily life to be given, guided, guarded, and energized by the grace of God. To live in grace is to flow in the Spirit.

> God's plan isn't just for us to be *saved* by grace — it's for us to *live* by grace.

We've now come to the most basic idea of this book (if you don't get anything else from reading these pages, please get this!): *The only way to become the person God made you to be is to live with the Spirit of God flowing through you like a river of living water.* The rest of this chapter will give a clear picture of what it looks

The only way to become the person God made you to be is to live with the Spirit of God flowing through you like a river of living water.

like to live from one moment to the next in flow with the Spirit — not in following rules or trying harder — so you'll receive the power to Really Live as the me God made you to be.

» Flowing with Life

In the book of John, the picture Jesus uses for life in the Spirit is a river. Rivers are mentioned 150 times in Scripture, often as a picture of spiritual life — and for good reason. Israel was basically a dry and dusty desert, so a river is life. A river is grace. We don't know much about the garden of Eden, but we do know this — a river ran through it.

> A river watering the garden flowed from Eden. (Genesis 2:10)

If a river flows, life blooms. If a river dries up, life dies. So it is with you and the Spirit. The first human being was just a lump of clay until God breathed into him the "breath of life." (In Hebrew the word for *breath* is the same word used for *spirit*.) One of the signs that you're in the flow of the Spirit is a sense of God-given vitality and joyful aliveness overflowing in you.

When our son was three years old, he wanted to pour his own glass of milk out of a very full carton. Nancy was hesitant; we had three small children, and spills were a way of life. But our son was so set on it that she couldn't say no, although she did warn him to be careful. His little hands picked up the heavy gallon container, and the milk went gushing into the glass — but wonder of wonders, it stopped just in time. The glass wasn't just full; the milk crowned the top of it. Not a drop was spilled. *Gloria in excelsis.*

But then Johnny was so excited that he grabbed the glass and swung it exuberantly from the counter to the table. The spillover was tremendous.

When someone bumps into me, what spills out of me shows everyone what's inside of me. Paul spoke of people being "full of the Spirit," and the spillover effect was amazing. Jesus told his followers that when the Spirit arrived, they would receive power. When the Spirit flows in you, you're given power to become the person God designed.

You become ... you-ier.

» In Flow with the Presence of God

What if God really is at work in every moment, everywhere? What if your job is just to jump into the river? What if your job is to figure out, from one minute to the next, how to stay in the flow? How to keep yourself aware of God's Spirit so that rivers of living water flow through your belly, through the core of your being?

The apostle Paul gives a simple command, and it pretty much simplifies things: "Do not quench the Spirit." The Spirit is already at work in you. Jesus says that if you've come to him, if you're a follower of his, the Spirit is there. The Spirit is bigger than you ... stronger than you ... more patient with your failures and your gaps and your inadequacies and your pretending than you. The Spirit is committed to helping you 24/7. So Paul says, in a sense, your only job is not getting in the Spirit's way. Just *don't quench the Spirit.*

» Just Plunge In!

The Holy Spirit is always ready to guide you toward God's best version of yourself. Of course, a lot of times I don't want to be guided! I want to blow up at somebody or be greedy or lie to get out of trouble. I want to quench the Spirit. It'll take time and wisdom to re-form old habits. But the Spirit of God is persistent. All that's needed in any moment is a sincere desire to be submitted to the

Spirit's leading. We don't need to worry about God's response; a sincere heart never needs to fear that God is upset.

A few years ago I was traveling on back roads in a part of the country I'd never been before. When I got my rental car, the guy at the counter said to me, "Along with this car, if you want, you can also get a little box, a guidance system." A GPS is a fabulous thing. I love how after you punch in your destination, a voice tells you how to get to wherever it is you're going.

"Do you want to add this to the car?" he asked.

My immediate response was, "No. I'm not going to pay for that. I can find where I'm going without that."

But when I went out to the parking lot, I couldn't even find my rental car! I couldn't remember what stall it was in, and I had to go back and tell the smiling man behind the counter that I wanted the GPS after all.

With this particular unit, the voice was British. (I think I know why: Go back and read the previous sentence in your best British accent. See how much smarter you sound?) And it was also a woman's voice because, well ... same thing.

So I'm driving along, and the GPS voice says, "Turn left." So I turned left. And eventually, after following the voice's instructions, I got to where I was supposed to go.

Likewise, to live in the flow of the Spirit means doing what Jesus says. I'll still mess up a lot—don't get me wrong. Since I'm not perfect, I need his power. So I'll pray, "God, with your help and as best I can, I'll do what you say. I'll give you my life, my time, my obedience."

There's something else you need to know—I didn't tell the whole story about my GPS adventure. At one point while driving in this unfamiliar territory, I was quite sure the GPS voice was wrong. It said to go left, but I didn't go left. I went right because I *knew* it was wrong. Then, in a fascinating response, the GPS voice said, "Recalculating route. When safe to do so, execute a U-turn." But I *knew* the voice was still wrong ... so I unplugged the GPS.

And—would you believe it?—I got crazy lost! (Which my wife enjoyed immensely, by the way.) So we plugged the GPS back in, and do you know what the voice said?

I told you so, you little idiot. You think I'm going to help you now? There's no way. You rejected me. You just find your own way home!

Of course the voice didn't really say that.

And God isn't like that either. Instead, God says, "Here's the way home. Execute a U-turn as soon as you're ready to listen, as soon as you're ready to surrender." That's repentance.

Then God says, "Okay, now I'll bring you home." That's grace.

Jesus is the only one with reliable wisdom about how to live. He's the only one to bring forgiveness for your sin and mine. He's the only one to give any kind of realistic hope of conquering death. To all who approach him, Jesus is the thirst-quencher, the life-giver, the Spirit-bringer. No matter how wrongly you've erred in the past, if you're sincerely ready to listen to and obey God, *then you don't have to worry about God being mad at you and turning away from you forever.*

God isn't like that.

Chapter 4

Find Out How You Grow

When a young shepherd boy named David was getting ready to battle the giant Goliath, King Saul stepped in to help. (You can read it for yourself in 1 Samuel 17.) But King Saul made the mistake we so often make in other battles: He figured that whatever would be helpful to *him* would also be helpful to *David*. So King Saul—who stood "head and shoulders" above every man in Israel—dressed up David in his own armor, crowned him with his helmet, and armed him with his sword. David "tried walking around" in them, the Bible says, but it was no use. Saul—a grown man and warrior—was a size XXL; David—a teenager shepherd—was a size Small. Saul's things didn't work for David. Saul's helmet was too big, his sword was too heavy, and his armor only slowed David down.

Fortunately, David had enough smarts and courage to name the problem. "I cannot go in these," David said, "because I am not used to them." David had to set aside Saul's equipment and use what would help *him*—a sling, some stones, and quick feet—and

Saul ended up sending David with the best help he could give: "Go, and the LORD be with you."

The greatest battle of life is spiritual—the struggles with anger and greed and hatred and authority that keep me from living in the flow with God. How often in our spiritual lives do we get overloaded by using weapons that have helped someone *else* in the battle? We hear about how others pray, or read Scripture to start or end their days, or worship, or study, or serve—and we feel guilty if we don't do the same. We get frustrated because what works for someone else isn't so helpful to us. We're like David, trying to walk around in Saul's armor.

The apostle Paul said to "put on the full armor of God." (If you haven't read about it before, look up Ephesians 6:10–20 and check it out right now! I'll wait here.) It includes truth and peace and prayer and faith. Have no doubt; it will fit you. If David had gone into battle using Saul's armor, he would have lost. God knew what Saul needed. God knew what David needed. *And God knows what you need.*

For we are God's masterpiece. He has created us anew in Christ Jesus, so that we can do the good things he planned for us long ago. (Ephesians 2:10 NLT)

The Bible doesn't say you're God's *machine*; it says you're God's masterpiece. Machines are mass-produced; masterpieces are handcrafted. God didn't make you exactly like anyone else. Therefore, God's plan for shaping you isn't exactly like God's plan for shaping anyone else. If you try to follow a generic plan for spiritual growth, it'll only frustrate you. Paul said, "Where the Spirit of the Lord is, there is freedom."

It's time for you to stop walking around in Saul's armor. It's time to get free.

» The Freedom Way

What would grow a tulip would drown a cactus. What would feed a mouse would starve an elephant. Those things need light, food, air, and water—but in different amounts and conditions. The key is not treating every creature alike; it's finding the unique conditions that help each creature grow.

Imagine a doctor's office where every patient is told, "Take two aspirin and call me in the morning." If I have a headache, that's great advice; but if my appendix has just burst, I'll be dead before morning. Imagine a store that sells only one kind of shirt—one color, style, fabric, and size. There are no "one-size-fits-all" stores because God made people in different sizes.

If we really want to help others grow spiritually, we'll have to help them in ways that fit their wiring. Our great model for this is God himself because God always knows just what each person needs.

God had Abraham take a walk, Elijah take a nap, and Adam take the rap.

God gave Moses a 40-year time-out, David a harp and a dance, and Paul some ink and a scroll.

God wrestled with Jacob, read the riot act to Job, whispered to Elijah, warned Cain, and comforted Hagar.

Jesus was stern with the rich young ruler, compassionate toward the woman caught in adultery, patient with the disciples, stern with the scribes, gentle with the children, and gracious with the thief on the cross.

God never grows two people the same way. God is a handcrafter, not a mass-producer.

Now it's your turn.

God has existed from eternity, but God has never had a relationship with you before—the *you* God wants you to be. God wants to do a new thing with you. The problem many Christians face when it comes to spiritual growth is that they listen to so-called experts talk about what they do in life and then believe that's exactly what they're supposed to do as well. When the expert advice doesn't work for them, they feel guilty and inadequate; they often give up.

God has a unique plan for the me God wants me to be. It won't look exactly like God's plan for anyone else, which means it'll take freedom and exploration for me to learn how God wants to grow me. *Spiritual growth is handcrafted, not mass-produced. God does not do "one-size-fits-all."*

When Jesus prayed for his disciples, he didn't pray, "May they all have identical devotional practices"; he prayed, "Father, may they be one with you." The main measure of your devotion to God isn't your devotional life—it's simply your life.

Spiritual growth is handcrafted, not mass-produced. God does not do "one-size-fits-all."

Trying to grow spiritually without taking who you are into account is like trying to produce athletes on an assembly line. If you train an 80-pound gymnast and a 300-pound linebacker exactly the same way, you'll end up with two useless 190-pound former athletes.

A frequent problem in the way we talk about spiritual growth is that there's not much spirit in it—God's Holy Spirit, that is. Only God makes things grow, and that growth isn't always predictable and doesn't always look the same.

What, then, do I need to know in order to learn how God wants to help me grow?

» What Brings Me Life?

If you're looking for a conversation stopper, try asking people this question: *How are your spiritual disciplines going?* Most of us would think of a short list of activities that fall in the "I *ought* to do this. But I don't do it as much as I should, so it makes me feel guilty just thinking about it" category. So here's a different question—maybe even a better one: *What do you do that makes you feel fully alive?*

Maybe you feel alive when taking a long walk at sunset. Maybe it's reading a great book and pondering its ideas and use of language. Maybe it's having a talk with a few close friends next to a bonfire (along with lots of laughter). Maybe it's watching a movie or a play that really inspires you. Maybe it's taking a long run or bike ride. Maybe you love to play an instrument. Maybe you come alive when pursuing a hobby.

Spiritual disciplines are no different: They're simply activities that make you more fully alive by the Spirit of Life.

Spiritual disciplines are simply activities that make you more fully alive by the Spirit of Life.

Of course, that's not equivalent to "doing whatever feels good in the moment." Spending too much time in front of a video game or eating too much food or experimenting with some dangerous activity may feel good for the moment, but those things don't lead us toward life. Eventually they lead to guilt, addiction, or regret.

The things that bring us life also aren't necessarily "what feels comfortable." Giving away money or confessing sin may feel difficult or scary at first, but later on we know we did the right thing.

We often assess how "spiritual" we are by how much we're pursuing our twisted sense of "what counts" toward spiritual growth instead of by our fullness of life. Sharing generously, listening to someone patiently, eating gratefully, thinking quietly, playing happily—they all count! *Every* moment is a chance to live in the flow of the Spirit.

No relationship can last if it's built purely on "should," either. My family, my friends—even my dog—don't want me to be with them only because I think I *should.* Because they love me, they give me freedom; and in that freedom my desire to be with them grows.

Likewise, where the Spirit is, there is freedom. It might seem strange, but when I think of God giving me freedom from the staleness of too many "shoulds," I find that my love and admiration for God grows. I want to be around a God like that!

The kind of spiritual growth that *lasts* happens when I actually *want* to do what I *ought* to do. This means I have to change how I think about what "counts" as spiritual—because what makes an action spiritual isn't the action itself; it's whether or not I do it with and through the Spirit.

» What's My Temperament?

Each human being has a temperament, or a "personality," which means certain practices will come more naturally for you than for others. Different temperaments aren't better or worse, they simply are. (Although I'd like to believe Jesus' personality was a lot like mine. Ha!) Everyone needs some time in solitude. But if your personality is kind of shy or introverted, then you have a greater need to withdraw from noise and people and tasks in order to be alone and quiet.

For me, the idea of going off to be alone almost always sounds appealing. However, time alone almost never happens by accident. It seems there's constantly something going on to distract me. I have to *choose* solitude, and the simplest way is to take my calendar, find a day in the future when I have no commitments, and block it off to go where I'd love to be—out in nature or at a retreat center or even just walking around the block.

People often wonder how long they should be in solitude. The great news is that you can experiment because spiritual practices are about freedom. If you've never done it before, just start with 15 minutes or so. After you've tried it a few times, you might be surprised how helpful it is—and how long you can spend time with God.

If you're more of an outgoing and social person, the idea of spending an hour by yourself might sound like a nightmare. But try it for 15 minutes anyway. Remember, though, that this isn't about the amount of time you spend in solitude; it's about the Spirit. Even if you're an introvert and love solitude, it doesn't mean you're more spiritual than your extroverted friend who's more naturally drawn to people and conversations and parties. If you're an extrovert, you may actually have a head start on loving people, since you're naturally attracted to those kinds of situations.

One guy I know is both super-outgoing and a deep feeler. He's in the flow of the Spirit best when he's neck-deep in the soul struggles of another human being. Even though he's trying to help someone else, it's in those conversations when his own soul feels alive. He found he needs to have conversations like this a lot.

Some people have personalities that crave regularity, order, and closure. If this is you, then having set times for prayer and lists of whom and what you're praying for might keep you connected to God. I know a woman who could show years of lists of prayers and years of lists of answers, and those lists are priceless to her. But if your temperament craves change, your prayer life is never going to look like that. You may have tried and then given up on the lists, feeling guilty. But it's not because you don't love God—it's just because you're not a list maker!

God wants to fill you with life, and you can't get filled up when you're too busy with an activity that drains you. Spontaneous people are capable of as much love as well-organized people—they're just messier. I know a guy who goes for walks a lot and turns his walks into times of prayer. For him, walking around gives his eyes something different to look at, and that helps his mind stay focused.

» What's My Learning Style?

Thankfully, spiritual growth isn't limited to people who enjoy school because God also wired us to learn in different ways. One guy is really bright and devoted to God, but he hates to read. Because of that, spiritual-growth practices that require a lot of reading won't help him. He has a huge capacity for growth, and he's a really sharp guy; he's just not a reader. He learns by listening. He learns from conversations and hearing someone talk.

Others learn mainly by doing. For example, if I try to assemble something, I'll read the instructions seven times before trying to put Tab A into Slot B. But my friend Sam is a hands-on guy. He'll try to build a nuclear power plant without looking at the directions first. Trial-and-error is the way he learns best (which is great, as long as he's not packing *my* parachute). For Sam, listening to a talk will never be his primary path to growth. An hour of doing, however, is worth 10 hours of listening.

learning styles

Visual — (learn best by seeing)

Auditory — (learn best by hearing)

Tactile — (learn best by doing)

Oral — (learn best by saying)

Social — (learn best in groups)

Logical — (learn best in linear process)

Imaginative — (learn best through art, story, and image)

Another friend of mine, Lee, learns best when her emotions are deeply engaged. She'll be impacted the most by information wrapped up in imagination, art, and other people. Her husband, Wendell, on the other hand, has an emotion only about once a decade. Deep emotion actually interferes with his learning.

You have a natural love for learning, but you have a natural *style* for learning as well. If someone reads the Bible more often than you do, that doesn't necessarily mean that person loves God more than you do — that person may just love reading more than you do. So try different styles of learning to see which fit you best.

Your path to growth won't be quite like anyone else's. It will be unique. It will be you-ier. It won't always be easy. But there's one decision that's always possible — that will always help you grow — and we'll take a look at that now.

Chapter 5

Surrender: The One Decision That Always Helps

There is a God. It is not you.

This is the beginning of wisdom. At first it looks like bad news because I'd like to run the world. I'd like to satisfy all my desires. I'd like to have my own way. But once we think about it, this idea turns out to be very good news.

It means that someone far wiser and more capable than us is running the show. It's God's job to be God; it's my job to learn to let God be God. The Bible says, "The fool has said in his heart, 'There is no God.'" I suppose the even bigger fool looks at himself in the mirror and thinks, *Now* there *is a god!* Way back in the first book of the Bible, Adam and Eve were tempted by the idea that they could "be like God." Real life, however, begins when I die to the false god—me.

Jesus said that out of our bellies can flow rivers of living water. The one decision needed in order for that to happen is to *surrender* myself to God. Give myself up to God. Even when I'm not exactly sure what to do, I can put my life in God's hands. To do this, we'll have to face our greatest fears.

» Who Will Drive Your Life?

Some of you can clearly remember when you first learned to drive — it happened only a few months or years ago. Or maybe you're looking forward to learning how to drive. It's an amazing, exciting thing! Except maybe not so much for parents . . . of which I am one.

When my kids learn to drive, I'm handing over the keys — literally and figuratively. They're moving from the passenger's seat to the driver's seat. Up until then, I did all the driving; I chose the destination, route, and speed. I was in control.

But we live in a neighborhood with twisty, winding streets, and whatever driving route I take — even if it's three blocks away — someone in my family evaluates it. "Why are you going this way? This is the long way! You should have gone the other way." And then I have to tell them this car is *my car.* These keys are *my keys.* This way is *my way.*

What can I say? In my family, everybody wants to drive.

It's the same way for most of us in life — deep down, we all want to be in control of our circumstances. Still, many of us find Jesus pretty handy to have in the passenger's seat whenever we require his services.

> *Jesus, there's a health problem in my family, and I need your help.*
> *Something hard is going on at school, and I'd like it to be different.*
> *I'm feeling fearful, and I want you to give me peace of mind.*
> *I'm feeling sad, and I'd like a little hope.*

But Jesus doesn't want to be a passenger — just like us, he wants to drive. The difference is that Jesus drives infinitely better than any of us can do. Even so, oftentimes we're not so sure that we want Jesus driving because if Jesus is behind the wheel, then we aren't in control anymore. When I let Jesus drive, I'm no longer in charge of my ego. I no longer have the right to satisfy every self-centered ambition. I'm not in charge of my mouth anymore. I don't get to gossip, flatter, sweet talk, slam, lie, curse, rage, cheat, intimidate, manipulate, or exaggerate anymore. Now my mouth is *his* mouth. Now my life is *his* life.

So I get out of the driver's seat. I hand over the keys to Jesus. And . . . I'm still absolutely engaged. In fact, I'm more alive than ever before. But it's not my life anymore. It's his life.

Does that sound like an exaggeration? It's not. Does it sound scary? It's actually better!

The key is surrender. Jesus is very clear on this point: *There's no way for a human being to come to God that doesn't involve surrender.*

Surrender isn't the same thing as being meek or tame. God's will for your life involves bold creativity, making choices, and taking initiative. Surrender doesn't mean being a doormat. It doesn't mean you accept circumstances like you're a victim. It often means fighting to challenge the norm. It doesn't mean you stop using your mind, asking questions, or thinking critically. This kind of surrender is definitely not a crutch for weak people who cannot handle life.

There's no way for a human being to come to God that doesn't involve surrender.

Instead, surrender is the glad and voluntary acknowledgment that there is a God and it is not me. God's purposes are wiser and better than our desires. Jesus doesn't come to rearrange the outside of our lives the way we want them to be. He comes to rearrange the inside of our lives the way God wants.

In surrender, I let go of my life. It's a revolution of the soul in which I take myself out of the center of the universe and put God there. (Which only makes sense—I was never in the center of the universe to begin with, and God was always there.) I yield to my Creator. I offer obedience. I do what God says. I'm not driving anymore.

When spirituality gets discussed in our culture, there are some messages from the Bible that everyone really likes hearing:

"No matter how much you mess up, God still loves you." Everybody digs that one.

"You are so busy and exhausted — God wants you to be rested and refreshed." That sounds great, too.

But what about these?

"You need to surrender. You are sinful and stubborn. You are self-centered and selfish, and your ability to recognize your own sin is blinded by the way you lie to yourself. You need to submit your heart, you need to confess your sin, you need to *surrender.*"

Jesus doesn't come to rearrange the outside of our lives the way we want. He comes to rearrange the inside of our lives the way God wants.

Surrender is a hard word.

I'll name one person who I know for sure doesn't like to hear that: *Me.*

» Why Surrender?

When our favorite quarterback throws a winning touchdown pass, when our favorite batter hits a game-winning home run, or when we ace a big exam, or when a guy or girl we like sends us a text message, we all experience a reflexive response with our bodies — we raise our hands high. During such times it's simply our instinct to stretch our hands toward heaven in a posture of victory and celebration.

There is another posture, however, that shows surrender: Kneeling. When a subject comes before his king, what does he do to humble himself? He kneels to show he's in the presence of his master.

Exalted high in victory. Bent low in surrender. The two postures may seem opposite, but Jesus said that if you want to experience victory, you have to start in surrender. Surrender brings power, and the need to surrender is totally tied to Jesus' offer of living in the flow of the Spirit. You get that spiritual power through the act of surrender; you receive freedom through submission.

Another gift of surrender is peace. If I live in the illusion that I am God, I'll drive myself (and everybody else) crazy with my need for control. When I surrender I don't let go of just my will; I also give up the idea that I'm in charge of *outcomes*.

"the nature of the will"

In a series of brilliant experiments, a psychologist named Roy Baumeister has studied the nature and limits of willpower. One key question was, *Once you apply your willpower — say, by resisting temptation for five minutes — does that make your willpower* stronger, weaker, *or* unchanged *for the next few minutes?*

Baumeister had certain people in the experiment apply willpower by resisting the temptation to eat delicious, fresh, warm, gooey chocolate chip cookies — eating only radishes instead. Another set of people in the experiment didn't have to resist eating cookies. Then everybody in the experiment was assigned complex math problems to solve — problems that were actually *impossible* to solve — so the researchers could measure how long people will exercise willpower to persevere in frustration.

The people who had to resist eating chocolate chip cookies gave up on problem-solving much more quickly than the other subjects did. In other words, our willpower is easily exhausted. We can use our wills to override our habits for a few minutes, but our habits will always beat willpower alone in the long run.

Deep change takes more than willpower. It requires God renewing our minds. It requires surrender.

tasks that require the will

- ≈ Making decisions (which is why taking a test wears us out)
- ≈ Maintaining an image
- ≈ Resisting temptation
- ≈ Persisting in a difficult task
- ≈ Breaking a habit (chewing your nails, overeating, and so on)
- ≈ Surrender

Amazingly, the one act of the will that *produces* energy rather than *drains* energy is surrender. Surrender actually refills our vitality. So try praying a prayer of surrender as you think of it throughout the day. Something like this:

"Father, today I gladly place my life in your hands . . ."

- ≈ When I wake up
- ≈ When I face a decision
- ≈ When I disagree with somebody
- ≈ When I'm tempted
- ≈ When I want to give up
- ≈ When I get mad

» The Action of Surrender

Sometimes I can *feel* devoted to God, but when it comes time to act, my surrender is only skin-deep.

Then I have to decide, *Will I surrender when it means doing something uncomfortable?* If it were comfortable, then it wouldn't be surrender.

One of the most amazing teachings of the Scriptures is that through the life of Jesus, God knows what it means to surrender. Before his crucifixion Jesus knelt in the garden of Gethsemane and prayed, "Let this cup pass from me: nevertheless not as I will, but as thou wilt." And just as Jesus' surrender to the pain of death led to his rising from the dead, so it does for his followers.

The only way to victory is through surrender.

So remember: Jesus is an absolutely skilled leader. When you wake up in the morning, you can feel completely confident in saying, "Okay, Jesus—today you lead, and I'll follow. My whole life is in your hands.

"You lead.

"I'll follow."

PART THREE

renewing my mind

Chapter 6

Let Your Desires Lead You to God

Two really athletic nine-year-olds start taking swimming lessons.

One begins because she's seen the Olympic games and wants more than anything in the world to win a gold medal when she grows up. She pictures herself on the podium; she surrounds herself with Olympic pictures; she listens to the national anthem every day.

The other kid starts lessons because her dad wants her to.

Which one is more likely to make it to the Olympics?

The one swimming for her dream.

Two 18-year-olds each have a goal to save $10,000.

One of them has a dream to buy a used sports car that he loves, that he's wanted since he was 12, and that will mean a new independence.

The other is saving because he thinks he should.

Who do you think will reach $10,000 first—and be willing to keep track of his expenses, eat cheaply, and buy less stuff at the mall?

The one saving for his dream.

In Genesis we learn that Jacob fell in love with Rachel so deeply that he agreed to work for her dad for seven years so he could marry her. "So Jacob served seven years to get Rachel, but they seemed like only a few days to him because of his love for her."

Who would regard seven years of work as just a couple of days?

The one working for his dream.

There's no power in life like got-to-have-it desire.

When Jesus described life with God, he told stories about got-to-have-it desire. He said it's like a man who finds a treasure buried in the field and excitedly sells everything he owns to buy the field because he had to have the treasure.

When people listened to Jesus, some of them had this desire awakened in them. They saw how Jesus lived his life. His peace, his courage, and his wisdom were like giant magnets pulling them in. Sooner or later the thought would go off in their brains, *I've gotta have what he has.*

But too often we're told that we *should* desire God above all things without being told *how*. We can't muster up desire on command. So if your spiritual want-to factor wobbles now and then, keep reading.

» You and Your Like-o-Meter

We evaluate most every experience or event with what a psychologist named Jonathan Haidt calls a "like-o-meter." Your like-o-meter was running the day you were born. Babies' taste receptors are pretty well developed, so for them the like-o-meter usually involves what goes into their mouths: "Like it—gotta have more" or "Hate it—get it out of here." As you continue to grow up, everything registers on your like-o-meter without you having to think about it. Every sound you hear, every conversation you're a part of, and every bite you eat either rates on the plus side or the minus side of your like-o-meter scale.

People also register somewhere on your like-o-meter. In the briefest of conversations, you'll find yourself leaning toward some people. Something inside of you says, *I like this person. This is a good conversation.* And other people will register negatively on your scale. You probably won't say, "Hey buddy, right now you're about a negative seven on my scale. And if you keep talking, you'll sink even lower." But an evaluation process is always going on. So here's a question to consider:

Do you like God?

That may sound like a strange question, and I don't mean to appear disrespectful about God—that's not what this is about. But when push comes to shove, if I don't like being with God, then I simply won't choose to be with God very much. It's good to be honest about this because if you don't like God, there's no use trying to fake out God.

The point isn't to make you feel guilty that you *should* want God more. "Should" simply doesn't have the power to get you there.

» The Little Engine That "Should"

"Should" is a kind of backup engine. I need to have this part of me because sometimes I must do things simply because I should. In most cases "want" eventually wears down to "should." (But then again, if I'm running in a marathon, it doesn't matter at mile marker 23 whether I feel like I *should* finish the 26.2 miles—I'll only finish because I *want* to finish.)

Spiritual growth doesn't mean a life spent doing what I *should* do instead of what I *want* to do. It means getting to the point where I actually want to do what I should do. When people come to understand how good God is, they *want* him. They don't just love him. They *like* him.

When we become aware of this, we feel guilty because our desire for God doesn't go deep enough—but we can't make ourselves desire God more by telling ourselves that we should. God is so gracious and patient, waiting for us to want him; and God is glad to work with this kind of honesty. That's why we're invited to "taste and see that the LORD is good."

Taste is an experimental word. It's an invitation from a confident chef. You don't have to commit to eating the whole thing; just try a sample—a *taste*. If you don't like it, you can skip the rest. But the chef is convinced that if you can be persuaded to take one bite, you'll want the whole enchilada.

» Use Your Authentic Desires to "Taste and See That the LORD Is Good"

When people enjoy what God has created, God's heart is pleased. But a lot of people think, *If I want to be spiritual, I have to avoid sin—and the best way to avoid sin is to get rid of desire altogether. If I just didn't want relationships or money or food or success or popularity, I'd be really spiritual because then I wouldn't sin.* But then you wouldn't be human, either. A slab of cement doesn't have to worry about weeds—but it'll also never be a garden.

When it's not wrecked by sin, desire is fabulous—fabulous because it's part of God's design. The psalmist says to God:

"You open your hand and satisfy the desires of every living thing. The LORD is righteous in all his ways and loving toward all he has made ... He fulfills the desires of those who fear him."

God is a desire-creating, desire-satisfying God. God made birds *with* the impulse to fly—they want to do it because God created them to fly. Dolphins swim because God made them with an instinct to swim. God doesn't plant wrong desires in his creatures.

God created desire, and it thrills God to fulfill desire. But I know that many of my desires are distorted by sin and need to be cleansed, purified, and retrained. This is what Jesus refers to when he says, "Whoever wants to be my disciple must deny themselves and take up their cross and follow me." We must say no to any desires that would keep us from living in the flow of the Spirit.

We must always be ready to sacrifice lesser desires for the sake of living greater lives.

> James speaks of the fulfillment of desire when he says, "Every good and perfect gift comes from above, from the Father of all lights who satisfies the desires of those who fear him . . ."

» Desires in Four Flavors

I'd like you to walk through four categories of desires and think about how they apply to you. As you do, be honest because on the surface these categories might not appear spiritual. Maybe you've always thought of them as having nothing to do with God; but if you let them, they can become part of living in the flow of the Spirit. The reality—the *spiritual* reality—is that each one of them has a God-designed part in our lives.

Material Desires

We all have *material desires*—desires attached to money and clothes and cars and "stuff." If we could get rid of every bit of our sin, we'd still desire material things because God created that stuff. It's a good thing to put beauty in your environment that speaks to your soul so you can experience the flow of the Spirit in your life. But if material desires choke your generosity, cause you to live in debt, or create constant dissatisfaction, then it's time to say no to them.

Is it bad to like cars? That's a material desire. If your desire for cars blocks your ability to be generous or puts you in debt, it's time to say no. But maybe God placed a desire for cars within you in order to help you do something with them someday—like fix them or design them. Isn't it possible that enjoying a car might be something you could do *with* God, as well? And when you're driving, you might say, "God, I invite you to be with me in this moment."

The Spirit could be flowing with you right there—*j-u-s-t* under the speed limit.

Achievement Desires

There haven't been many people in history more motivated by achievement than the apostle Paul. He was constantly moving, teaching, building, and motivating. He describes his life with word-pictures like, "I have fought the good fight, I have finished the race." God didn't take away Paul's desire to achieve; instead, he directed it so Paul could serve others.

Maybe you have a strong drive in school or in sports or in some other extracurricular activity. Maybe you just love to accomplish stuff. If your achievement desires are leading you to forget about prayer or prop yourself up or use others, however, then you need to redirect this part of yourself. But if that's not the case—if you find yourself growing in God and you have an inner fire to achieve under God's direction—then go ahead and achieve.

Use your ability to accomplish good for others. And when you're achieving, you'll know it's about more than just you. Every now and then stop and thank God that you get to do this; because as you achieve and feel joy in doing it, you're opening yourself up to the flow of the Spirit.

Relational Desires

In the Old Testament we read about the friendship between Jonathan and David. Even though Jonathan was the king's son (and in line to be the next king), he voluntarily gave up his power because he knew his friend David was God's choice to be king. Jonathan wanted to be a friend more than he wanted to be king. (Wow!)

We all have relational desires. Maybe you hunger for deep relationships but find they're difficult to navigate—and you get discouraged. When great friendships don't just fall into your lap, maybe you tend to give up. But great friendships don't just fall into our laps. Jonathan had to overcome unbelievable barriers to build his friendship with David—and there's a good chance that you will, too, in order to build a relationship like that. But you can.

If you're a really social person, don't hesitate to get groups of people together on a regular basis. You know that joy you feel when people are gathering and talk is flowing and laughter is booming and new friendships are building? That's straight from God. You can be God's instrument to help people connect with each other.

Physical Desires

Because your body was made by God, you also have appetites—desires to eat, to drink, to touch, to see, to feel, to hear, and to speak. *Physical* desires. The Old Testament is filled with commands for God's people to feast, eat, drink, celebrate, sing, dance, shout, and make music—all things we do with our bodies. These appetites, desires, and delights can then become ways of remembering how good our God is.

You learn to connect the gift—which you already love—with the Giver, whom you want to love more. You start with what you already like and work your way back to its source: God.

How do you "connect the dots," learning to connect the gift with the Giver?

≈ Take a minute at the beginning of the day to invite God to be with you.
≈ Intentionally say "thank you" to God in the midst of your enjoyment.
≈ Put pictures on your screensaver or in your locker of what enjoyably reminds you of God's goodness throughout your day.
≈ Use a "breath prayer" such as "Thank you for my body" or "Thank you for this friendship" to help you share your experience with God. A breath prayer is a simple one-sentence prayer (you can say it in one breath) that energizes the soul the way oxygen energizes the body.
≈ Chew on Bible passages that show God delighting in creatures and bodies and fulfilling desires. (Psalms 103 and 104 are great for this.)

Have you ever desired to be physically attractive? (I ask that question every once in a while in adult church services, but no one ever raises their hands. Hmm.) This needs to be kept in proper perspective, of course, because the writer of Proverbs does warn, "Like a gold ring in a pig's snout is a beautiful face on an empty head." Beauty of character is a greater good than exterior beauty—but God *did* create our bodies. So can we get real? God made us with a love of beauty.

It's a good thing to eat food you love to eat, wear clothes you love to wear, listen to music that makes you feel glad, and then thank God that he gave you your body so you can see and hear and touch and laugh and dance. As you open yourself to the flow of the Spirit in your physical desires, you begin to love God more and more—not because you should or because it's commanded, but because when you get to know God, you just can't help it.

You see, I'm a dad. I'm not a heavenly Father like God; but still, I'm a dad. And hardly anything gives me more joy than making my kids happy. When their faces light up because I've given them things they really wanted, that's the best feeling in the world. Of course, I don't want them to become selfish, so I decide when it's better for them to do without things they want—but I just love it when I can give to them, and they react with such delight.

Imagine how much more joy God feels when giving us things we want, and we demonstrate our delight.

Chapter 7

Think Great Thoughts

One recent Saturday night our house was invaded by an odor that burned our nostrils so badly that we had to get out. We figured it was a gas leak, so we called the gas company and the fire department. As it turned out, a skunk had gotten very close to our house.

I made a few phone calls, but no exterminator would come look for a skunk. So we figured the problem would go away on its own. Most of the odor faded, and what stayed behind we got used to. It didn't bother us—until someone visiting our house would come in and say, "It smells like a *skunk* around here."

A week later, I was traveling when my family called to say the skunk had struck again. I had to find someone who specialized in the ways of the skunk—a "skunk whisperer." The man discovered that we had two live skunks and one dead one residing in the crawl space under our house. It cost a lot to get the skunks removed, but it was worth it.

You cannot get rid of the skunk odor without getting rid of the skunk.

Our sense of smell has a unique power to stir up emotions, and our feelings are kind of like smells. Our positive feelings—joy, excitement, gratitude—thrill us like the scent of chocolate chip cookies just out of the oven. Negative feelings—sadness, worry, anger—can make us want to evacuate our lives. When they hit, our mood dips, we lose energy, God seems distant, prayer seems pointless, sin looks tempting, and life looks depressing.

But our feelings never tumble down on us at random. As a general rule, our emotions flow from our thoughts. When we're discouraged, we tend to think discouraging thoughts. When we're worried, we tend to think anxious thoughts. These thoughts become so automatic that—like the lingering skunk odor—after a while we don't even notice we're thinking them. We get used to what's sometimes called "stinking thinking."

The way we live will inevitably be a reflection of the way we think. True change always begins in our minds. The good news is God *can* change our thinking. What makes people the way they are—what makes you *you*—is mainly the way they think.

> Let God transform you into a new person by changing the way you think. (Romans 12:2 NLT)

Becoming the best version of yourself, then, rests on one simple instruction: *Think great thoughts!* People who live great lives are people who habitually think great thoughts. Their thoughts move them toward confidence, love, and joy. Trying to change your emotions by willpower alone and without allowing the stream of your thoughts to be changed by the flow of the Spirit is like disinfecting the house of the skunk smell while the skunks are still living in your basement. But God can change the way we think, and in this chapter we'll look at two ways we can open ourselves up to God's work: Learning to monitor what happens in our minds and then resetting our minds to better frequencies.

It's time to go after the skunks in our minds.

» Learn to Monitor Your Mind

Our thought patterns become habits—like brushing our teeth. After a while we don't even stop to consider them. We get so used to harsh thoughts or anxious thoughts or selfish thoughts that we don't even notice what we're thinking about.

The spiritual life starts with paying attention to our thoughts, which is why David prayed in Psalm 139, "Search me, God, and know my heart; test me and know my anxious thoughts." God knows our thoughts better than we do, and he'll help us learn what's going on in our minds from one moment to the next.

As I monitor my mind, I'll notice many thoughts that are unwelcome visitors: I get anxious. I think the worst. I get jealous of somebody. But I'll also start to recognize what kinds of thoughts the Spirit flows in. In the writings of Paul, we get a great framework for understanding which thoughts and attitudes come from the Spirit: "The mind controlled by the sinful nature is death, but the mind controlled by the Spirit is life and peace."

Take any thought, especially those that feel heavy or that you find yourself turning over and over in your mind, and ask, *In what direction do those thoughts lead me? Are they leading me toward life—toward God's best version of me? Or in the other direction?*

This is where grace comes in. Even though there are bits of pain in these heavy thoughts, they don't paralyze me. They bring energy. They're true, and they give me ground to stand on. I realize that if I can keep my mind centered on these thoughts, right feelings and actions are likely to flow out of them. The prophet Isaiah writes that we'll be kept in perfect peace if our minds are *stayed* on God. This is living in the flow of the Spirit.

Here's an exercise for supervising your mind. Read through the list of words below, which represent the main patterns of our thinking. As you read through the list, consider your own mental habits and how other people experience you. Then select three words that express the patterns that tend to characterize your thinking. Ask one or two people who know *and* love you to go through the same list and choose three words that they believe best characterize you.

Grateful Curious Stubborn

Defensive Hopeful Angry

Self-focused Hesitant Determined

Unsatisfied Stressed Focused

Creative Courageous

Learn to become aware of the flow of your thoughts without trying too hard to change them. Toddlers learning to walk will learn from their falls—but without making judgments that can paralyze them. (You never hear them say, "I've fallen down again! What an awkward dork I am! I'm just going to crawl the rest of the day! I don't deserve to walk!") Learning to walk in the Spirit takes at least as much grace and strength as learning to walk on two legs, and the Spirit will always lead us toward God's best version of ourselves.

» Learn to Set Your Mind

You can't stop thinking wrong thoughts by trying harder not to think them. But you can do something else: You can "set your mind"—for the most basic power you have over your mind is choosing what you pay attention to. At any moment—including right now—I can direct my thoughts one way ... or another. That explains why two people can be in the same set of circumstances and have completely different experiences.

A friend sent me these "entries" from a dog's diary and a cat's diary to illustrate the difference that a mindset can make:

Excerpts from a Dog's Diary:

8:00 am—Dog food! My favorite thing!
9:30 am—A car ride! My favorite thing!
9:40 am—A walk in the park! My favorite thing!
10:30 am—Got scratched and petted! My favorite thing!
12:00 pm—Lunch! My favorite thing!
1:00 pm—Played in the yard! My favorite thing!
3:00 pm—Wagged my tail! My favorite thing!
5:00 pm—Doggie treats! My favorite thing!
7:00 pm—Got to play ball! My favorite thing!
8:00 pm—Wow! Watched TV with the people! My favorite thing!
11:00 pm—Sleeping on the bed! My favorite thing!

Excerpts from a Cat's Diary:

Day 983 of my captivity. My captors keep ridiculing me with bizarre, little dangling objects. The only thing that keeps me going is my dream of escape.

Two creatures, identical circumstances, but totally different experiences. What's the difference? It's a way of thinking. Gratitude is one mindset; demand (or entitlement) is the opposite.

Setting your mind is like setting a thermostat—it creates a target for the temperature. Once you set a thermostat, the heating and air conditioning adjust in relation to the weather. It's a constant process, but the goal is for the system to create a livable climate. So it is with our minds. Many people try to tell themselves to *stop* thinking negative thoughts—which immediately brings to mind the same thoughts they're trying to stop thinking.

Set your minds on things above, not on earthly things. (Colossians 3:2)

Those who live in accordance with the Spirit have their minds set on what the Spirit desires. (Romans 8:5)

There's a better way.

My friend Danny went spelunking in Iowa (*spelunking* being the fancy word for "exploring caves"). The guide took Danny deep underground, and then he said he'd lead Danny through a passageway and on into a spectacular chamber. The passageway was small enough that Danny had to stoop at first. Then as it grew still smaller, he had to get on his hands and knees. Eventually the only way to move forward was by lying on his back and pushing his body with his feet. Then the ceiling became so low that when he filled his lungs with air, he couldn't move at all! He had to stop, inhale, exhale, and only then was his chest low enough to allow him to move. By this point it was physically impossible to back out. If the passageway had gotten any smaller, they would have lain there and died in that cave.

Danny is a skydiving, mountain-climbing, hang-gliding thrill-seeker, but there in that cave he felt absolute panic. He was terrified. He tried fighting his fear, but he kept picturing his dead body rotting in the cave. Finally, he told his guide he was about to lose it, and the guide said, "Danny, close your eyes and listen to my voice. I'll keep talking calmly and guide you through this. We will be okay. I've been here before. I will get you to the other side. But you need to listen to my voice. It won't work for you to let your thoughts run wild. Just focus on my voice."

Danny did so. What stopped his panic and fear wasn't trying hard to quit thinking fearful thoughts; it was listening to another voice—a voice he could trust.

What voice do you listen to when you're in a situation that feels like that cave—it's dark, the ceiling is low, and you can't back out? The Spirit really wants to flow in our minds all the time. One reason why people have found memorizing Scripture helpful is that it helps us listen to the voice of our Guide when we're in tough situations. I might mess up, but the Spirit reminds me that I'm still God's beloved child. I might get criticized, but the Spirit reminds me that truth and grace are always my friends.

God's gift of your mind is unbelievably generous. Before you were born, your body produced about 200 billion neurons, giving you the power to think and react. You had such a ridiculous amount of riches that by the time you were born, you killed off around 100 billion of those neurons, and you've never missed them. During the period of time starting while you were still in your mom's belly and ending on your second birthday, your body produced 1.8 neuron connections *per second*. And you weren't even tired!

Your thoughts have incredible power over your life. Researchers have found that tennis players can improve their backhands just by rehearsing them *mentally*. Neurons are firing in your mind that will change you. Over time, those pathways between neurons get shaped in ways that are absolutely unique to you—and God has no intention of wasting them.

It's amazing how often people believe they're victims of whatever thoughts happen to be running through their heads. It's like they're passive spectators watching thoughts run across the screen with no control over what's on it.

But in the spiritual life, there's a deep battle being waged by the Evil One over the nature of the thoughts that run through your mind. The crucial freedom that you have—the freedom no one can take away—is the freedom to decide what your mind will dwell on. I "set my mind" to look for the presence and goodness of God in my life, the river of living water flowing out of my belly.

A great guy I know used to stop by a newsstand each morning to get a paper on his way to work. Every single day the worker behind the counter was a grouch, but this man would respond with consistent good humor and politeness. A friend who sometimes went with him to work asked him why he stayed so kind while this guy was always so rude. He replied, "Why should I let his unhappiness control my attitude?"

Somebody is serving me in the cafeteria. I don't notice her, as she's just a background character in the movie of my life. Then the Spirit intervenes. The thought occurs in my mind, *Pay attention. Look in her eyes. This is a person with a family, with hopes and dreams.* For a moment I come alive. I can tell her "thank you" and mean it. I can bless her—willing good for her before God. And the world moves a tiny little bit toward Really Living.

The Holy Spirit is flowing, wanting to renew your mind all the time—as if there's a little network called HSN (Holy Spirit Network). I can tune into the Holy Spirit at any moment. I can ask the Spirit to guide my thoughts.

I can pause and listen.

Joshua Bell just might be the world's finest violinist. His parents knew he was something special when he was only four years old and he stretched rubber bands to his dresser drawers and played classical tunes on them, adjusting their pitch by pulling the drawers in and out.

As an experiment, he played — unannounced — in a Metro station in Washington, D.C. The people who conducted this experiment were warned by experts that a crowd would certainly gather; they might need extra security. They were sure that tons of people would flock to this once-in-a-lifetime opportunity.

Joshua Bell brought his violin — a 1713 Stradivarius, which cost *millions* of dollars — and began to play the six most beautiful songs in his playlist. The world's greatest violinist playing the world's greatest music on the world's greatest instrument.

But no one stopped. A thousand people walked by. You can see it on YouTube. Children would tug on their parents' sleeves, but the adults were too preoccupied. Only one woman recognized him and stopped to listen. She gave him a bigger tip ($20) than the other thousand people put together. They were in a hurry, hurrying past Joshua Bell because they had other things to do.

Jesus said, "To what can I compare this generation?... 'We played the flute for you, and you did not dance.'"

The Master is still playing, but listening is optional. Those who have ears to hear, let them hear.

Chapter 8

Feed Your Mind Great Stuff

We once lived across the street from a couple who didn't get along. The husband was a security guard, but what he really loved was bodybuilding. He was strong, sarcastic, and selfish. His wife was small and shy—and angry.

He had to go to work every morning at six, and she got up at five to fix his lunch. We wondered why she did this for someone she was so mad at—until she explained that she was secretly packing his lunches with enough calories to put weight on Shamu the Killer Whale. She loaded what he thought were diet turkey sandwiches with butter and mayonnaise. She put extra sugar in his yogurt. He worked out a lot, but he could never understand why his body didn't look like the guys in the magazines.

He never knew she was filling him with lard when he wasn't looking.

Our bodies are constantly being formed by what goes into them. We might not like this truth, we may not pay attention to it, but we can't get away from it. The same rule applies to our minds.

Daily we're bombarded by a steady stream of messages from teachers, friends, *supposed* friends, people we date, the Internet, TV shows, iPods—and our own thoughts. Our minds will be shaped by whatever we feed them—and at the same time the Evil One will try to lard up our minds when we're not looking. He'll put depression in our thoughts at breakfast, sprinkle temptation in our minds during lunch, and slip us worry sandwiches when it's time for bed.

Satan will try to keep us from noticing what we're putting into our minds.

» A Really Alive Mind Feeds on Life-Giving Thoughts

If I want my mind to be full of life, I must pay attention to what it's focused on. One of the greatest gifts God has given the human race is Scripture—but we often turn it into a heavy load. Sometimes people ask me, "How many minutes a day am I supposed to read the Bible? Seven? Fifteen? What's the minimum I can read and not have God be mad at me?"

That's the wrong question! God isn't mad at us for not reading the Bible. No matter how much we read the Bible, God won't love us any more or less than he loves us right now. The question is, *What can we feed our minds so they can Really Live?*

Other people ask, "How much more information about the Bible am I supposed to know? What if I feel guilty because so many people know so much more about the Bible than I do?" But the reason to read the Bible isn't to fulfill a spiritual "duty" or to gain more knowledge; it's to get in the flow of the Spirit. So let's talk about the feeding of our minds—including how we use the Bible. But let's not try harder. Let's try differently.

"Blessed are those ... who delight in the law of the LORD and meditate on his law day and night. They are like a tree planted by streams of water, which yields its fruit in season and whose leaf does not wither—whatever they do prospers."

The phrase "meditate on his law day and night" may sound intimidating, unrealistic, or undesirable. Maybe you wonder, *How would I ever get any work done if I spent the whole day thinking about the Bible?* But that's not necessary. That's not the idea.

Somebody once said that if you can worry, you can meditate. Meditating is simply turning a thought over and over in your mind. When you get information that matters to you, you can't help meditating on it.

When I was in high school, a friend of mine told me about a girl who liked me. I couldn't believe it because this girl was *way* out of my league.

"This can't be true," I said.

"But it *is* true," my friend said. "I don't understand it either, but it's true."

That night my mind fixated on this thought: *She likes me.* I couldn't stop thinking about it. My mind just went there over and over. *She* likes *me*. So the next day, although I could hardly believe it was true, I called her up and asked her out.

It turned out it wasn't true.

But I had one really good night thinking about it. It was my *delight*; and what I delight in, I can't help thinking about.

What would it look like to delight in the law of the Lord? It certainly is something deeper than being thrilled about a bunch of rules in the Bible. It starts with a vision of being loved by God. And God is way out of my league. God is in the *perfection* league; I'm in the *sinful* league. This wonderful God—this mysterious, all-powerful, all-holy God—loves me! Sometimes this truth really clobbers us, and we can't stop thinking about it.

God loves *me*!

The psalmist is saying that he's actually found ways to carry thoughts of God's love and protection into his mental life—his inner flow—that make his whole life better. Being loved by God is so stuck in his brain that now it affects all his other thoughts as well.

Think about it like this: There are two ways of looking when it comes to a window. I can look *at* a window—in other words, notice the glass and see if there are any smudges or dust particles or bubbles in it. Or I can look *through* a window—in other words, view the world beyond it by using the pane as an opening to the world.

In the same way, sometimes I look *at* the Scriptures—in other words, I just read the words. But I also need to look at my world *through* the Scriptures—in other words, I should think about its story and ask questions. Thoughts of God's goodness, love, and peace stick in my mind because I'm reading the Bible through the viewpoint of God's constant care and presence.

» Free to Think about "Whatever . . ."

When the apostle Paul tells us how to feed our minds, he writes, "Whatever is true, whatever is noble, whatever is right, whatever is pure, whatever is lovely, whatever is admirable—if anything is excellent or praiseworthy—think about such things."

The key word in that command is *whatever*. We're now free—even commanded—to fill our minds with true thoughts wherever we find them. The Bible itself commands us to look beyond just the Bible to feed our minds.

Think for a minute about that phrase "whatever is lovely." Think of something that's "lovely" to you. A sunset. Music that makes you dance. Your pet. A sport you can't get enough of. The face of someone you love. Let your mind stay there for a minute. Give it all of your mental focus.

Guess what? You just obeyed God's command as found in the Bible. That "counts"! You just opened up your mind a bit to the flow of the Holy Spirit.

What makes your mind get drawn to what's true, noble, right, pure, lovely, admirable, excellent, and praiseworthy? Maybe it's an art class where you learn to see beauty you'd never noticed before. Maybe you're an athlete, and competition stirs you to admire the pursuit of excellence. What causes *your* mind to be drawn to the qualities God wants you to focus on?

God's desire is that your mind should regularly think noble, true, pure, and excellent thoughts. You have great freedom—*whatever*—to allow the Spirit to rewire your mind. As that happens the Holy Spirit's goal isn't to get you really good at covering up angry behavior. It's to help your mind have an increasing flow of Spirit-guided, life-producing thoughts and feelings.

The flow of the Holy Spirit is always right there. You don't have to wait for anything.

» How to Get Fed from the Bible

We're free to feed our minds from every good source, but there's no source like the Bible. It's a written eye-opener to who God is and what God wants for humans. No book is more significant. No book is more powerful.

And Scripture has never before been this easy to access—and harder to soak in. The thing people feel guilty about saying is that the Bible seems boring to them. This is both a serious problem and a very recent one. The ancient Greeks didn't even have a word for *boredom* in their language! We look at the ancient world, and they had no TV, no Internet, no movies, no iTunes, and almost no books—and we think of how boring it must have been.

But the ancients weren't bored. Instead, we're the ones who get bored. And why? Because our ability to focus our attention has been weakened.

Part of why delighting in the Scriptures is harder for us to do than for the ancients is that we have a lot more tempting options. When David was watching sheep, he had nothing more entertaining to do, so he wrote psalms, memorized them, and sang them. They shaped his mind. "The LORD is my shepherd; I shall not want . . ." The pasture he sat in became a hangout for God's kingdom.

In a world with so many *easy* options to amuse or distract our minds, we all have to learn to be fed by the Bible.

Read the Bible with Curiosity

We can learn a lot from the Bible if we just ask questions: *Who's the author of this book? Who was it written to? Is the writing a parable, instruction, a letter, or history? How would the people to whom the words were first written have understood it?*

A friend of mine, a pastor of a church in the Midwest, was teaching the children's sermon one Sunday. He quizzed the kids to see how much they knew about the Bible. "See that man with two stone tablets in his hand, standing on a mountain?" he asked, pointing to the stained-glass windows. "Can anyone tell me his name?"

"Moses," said one girl.

"Very good. How did you know?"

"Because the name underneath the man says, 'Moses.'"

My friend had looked at the window a hundred times, but he'd never seen the name.

Similarly, our brains are wired to focus in the face of newness and chill out when we're in familiar situations. This means that when we read Scripture, we'll be the most focused if we ask questions and look for something we hadn't noticed before.

One of the most important tools for reading Scripture is one we've always got with us—our imaginations. When you read a Bible story, take time to imagine the details. In John 21, for example, Jesus prepared a breakfast of fish over a charcoal fire when the disciples came in from fishing. So ask yourself, *What does the water sound like, slapping against the boat? What would it smell like—the charcoal fire and the fish sizzling in the pan?* I imagine the light of an early sunrise painted in the sky. *How does it feel to be Peter as Jesus calls his name? How would it feel if it were me—if I'd bailed on Jesus like Peter had?*

When I really get into the story, it comes alive, and God can speak to me in a new way through a passage I may have read many times before. It's a little like getting lost in the plot of a movie when you're sitting in a darkened theater. You can do this with Scripture, too, and it'll change the way you experience the Bible!

Read Scripture with Expectancy

Sometimes people bring energy to a crowd; sometimes they just show up. My wife used to head up a ministry to people in their 20s who were mostly single. I knew, even with my eyes closed, if I was in their presence just by the smell. (They smelled great.) In regular church services, with mostly old married people, no one cares how they smell. But when people are hopeful of meeting someone they might date, there's electricity in the air—and an aroma in the air. They're alive.

It's the same with God. If I really believe I can meet with God, I don't just show up—my mind is awake. I'm hoping and looking for something beyond myself. If my wife hands me the sports page to read, she doesn't care if I scan it casually. But if she hands me a long letter she's spent hours writing me for our anniversary, it's not time for a casual scan. I approach that reading with a different attitude.

I can't *make* myself be excited about reading the Bible, and it isn't wise to try.

But if I come to Scripture with an attitude of expectancy, that changes things.

Read the Scriptures the Way You Watch a Movie

Sometimes when a group gathers, one person mentions a movie that everyone has seen, and suddenly a discussion surrounding that movie comes alive. People talk about their reactions to the movie with a lot of energy. Nobody "tried hard" to watch the movie; instead, everybody was focused on it. But when it comes to the Bible, the conversations become unnatural. People get so concerned with making sure they get the "right" answer that everyone backs out of the conversation. What if we talked about the Bible like we talk about movies?

Sometimes Try Memorizing Scripture

I know: Memorization scares us. But I also know people who've memorized every episode of *The Simpsons* without really trying.

Before written languages were developed, memory was the only way to learn. In our day memorizing has gotten a bad name. But memorizing never makes our mind a duller place—just the opposite! When we've stored fantastically true words in our memory, our inner life is much better off than the inner life of someone who hasn't memorized those words.

When you see a verse that really hits you, write it on a card or sticky note. Then put it on a mirror in your bathroom, or inside your locker, or next to your bed. It'll help you learn and memorize that verse. (But if you learn and memorize better by listening, then listen to the Scripture verse being read on CD or on an iPod.)

Don't Just Read It . . . Do Something

A ferocious businessman once told the author Mark Twain that before he died he wanted to visit the Holy Land to climb Mount Sinai and read the Ten Commandments aloud. "I have a better idea," Twain said. "You could stay here in Boston and keep them."

In the same way, we'd rather debate about things we don't know than actually do the things we know we ought to do.

We'd rather debate about things we don't know than actually do the things we know we ought to do.

Usually our problem isn't ignorance; it's knowing enough but doing little or nothing about it.

It's not rocket science. *Just go do it.* Practice loving a difficult person or forgiving someone. Give away some money. Tell someone thank you. Encourage a friend. Encourage an enemy. Say, "I'm sorry." Worship God.

You already know what you need to know.

Don't debate about the little stuff. Just go practice the big stuff.

This is our challenge.

Be doers of the word, and not merely hearers.

We don't become doers through our own power, though. As we read the Scriptures, we must ask the Spirit to help us understand what to do as a result of reading them. We'll have never-ending chances to actually do what Jesus says. And when we forget or mess up, another chance will come along.

I was picking up a prescription at the pharmacy one Saturday afternoon before a church service. And because I was in a hurry, I'd called the night before to make sure it would be ready. But when I got there, the man behind the counter told me it wouldn't be ready until the next week. Apparently there was a mix-up between the medical people, the insurance people, and the pharmacy people.

"But I've got to have it," I replied, as I was scheduled to leave the United States the next day.

"Well, it's not ready," the clerk said.

"But the automated system told me last night that it would be ready today."

"There is a flaw in the automated system then," he told me.

All of a sudden I felt unbelievable anger well up inside me. *A flaw in the system?* I wanted to say, *There's a flaw in you!* I didn't say that, but with every gesture and tone I could dream up, I expressed annoyance and irritation with the man behind the counter. I didn't simply *feel* anger—I *wanted* to feel it. I wanted to make him feel wrong. I was amazed at my own ugliness.

When I got to my office at the church, I opened my Bible and read a single phrase—"Love one another." And then I had to call a friend to tell him there was an inner jerk inside of me who's scary.

After I got back from my trip, I went to the pharmacy to tell the man behind the counter that I was sorry for being so irritated and how much I appreciated his help.

And I was back in the flow.

Chapter 9
Never Worry Alone

When our daughters were three and five years old, we took them to a hotel with a swimming pool. Beforehand, we had a long, stern talk about the importance of water safety and the risk of drowning.

My talk may have been a little too effective.

As five-year-old Laura jumped into my arms, three-year-old Mallory slipped into the water from a sitting position on the edge of the pool. She was underwater for less than a second, but when I pulled her up, she was sobbing.

"I drowned!" she cried. "I drowned! I drowned!"

From her viewpoint, it was terrifying. From my viewpoint, however, it was actually kind of funny.

"No, honey," I replied with care. "You didn't drown. You were only underwater for a second. You're fine ... so let's not tell Mommy about this."

Mallory was never in danger. I knew that to be true even though she didn't. Her father was always watching her, and he was able to scoop her out of trouble at a moment's notice.

Similarly, Jesus knows that no situation on earth has the power to put us outside of God's care. We're always in the hands of our Father. So even when death comes for us, it will be like Mallory dipping into the pool. We'll come up saying, "I drowned! I drowned! I drowned!" And the Father will say to us, "I had you the whole time."

Try a thought experiment: *Imagine not being afraid anymore. Imagine facing school pressures or an irate teacher with inner calm. Imagine facing rejection and obstacles without giving in to discouragement. Imagine admitting the mistakes you've made but then moving confidently into the future. Imagine doing all of this with* God *as your partner and friend. Now imagine the people around you coming to you when they're frustrated or discouraged because they find that your peace of mind is contagious.*

The mind controlled by the Spirit is life and peace, and what you're imagining is your mind immersed in the Spirit's flow. There's a phrase that wonderfully describes the role the Spirit wants to play in our minds: *The Spirit is a calming friend.*

» God's Calming Friendship

A calming friendship works like this: A group of people at home or school faces a problem. One person after another hits the panic button, and pretty soon everyone is anxious. Everybody is starting to freak out. It's contagious. Then they notice someone among them who isn't afraid, someone who's fully aware of the problem but remains calm and able to think with quiet confidence. That new spirit then begins to spread. Everyone starts to calm down. That one person brings the gift of a calming friendship. It reassures everybody that things are going to be okay.

Jesus was napping in a boat when a storm came. Jesus' friends, the disciples, woke him because they were terrified by the coming storm. Then Jesus looked out at the storm and said, "Peace, be still." And it was.

Jesus' was a calming friendship. He carried peace with him. He didn't say, "If you follow me, you'll never have problems," because even Jesus faced big problems. When you think about it, Jesus was always getting himself into trouble. Eventually he got killed.

Peace doesn't come from finding a lake with no storms; it comes from having Jesus in the boat.

God doesn't want us to live in worry or fear. God wants us to live with bold confidence in his power. "For the Spirit God gave us does not make us timid, but gives us power, love and self-discipline." In the Bible God rarely sends people into situations where their comfort level is high. Instead God promises to be *with* them in their fear.

For the Spirit God gave us does not make us timid, but gives us power, love and self-discipline.

God told Abraham to leave everything familiar, go to a land he didn't know, and then God would use Abraham to give birth to a new nation that would change the world. Abraham went and a nation was born.

God told Moses to confront Pharaoh—the most powerful man on earth—and then God would use Moses' faithfulness to rescue God's people. Moses confronted and God delivered.

God told Joshua to be a strong and courageous leader when everyone else wanted to return to slavery, and God would go with them and give them the land. Joshua was strong and courageous, and God gave them the land.

Peace doesn't come from finding a lake with no storms; it comes from having Jesus in the boat.

Over and over we see this pattern repeated. David faced the giant Goliath, Daniel faced a den of lions—and always there was God in the middle of their fear.

a test to worry about

This is a little quiz adapted from Harvard researcher Edward M. Hallowell. Score yourself on each question from 0 (not at all) to 3 (definitely yes).

1. Do you wish you worried less?
2. Do worries sometimes pop into your mind and take over your thinking like annoying little gnats?
3. Do you find compliments or reassurance hard to accept?
4. Are you more concerned about what others think of you than you should be?
5. How much do you procrastinate? (Have you still not finished the last question?)
6. Do you avoid confrontation?
7. Do you ever feel compelled to worry that a certain bad thing might happen out of an almost superstitious feeling that if you don't worry about it, then the bad thing will happen; while if you do worry about it, your worrying might actually prevent the negative outcome?
8. Do you "worry about your worry"? Do you sometimes feel God is disappointed by your lack of faith?
9. Are you worried about what your score will be on this quiz?

If you scored a 0, you're either a remarkably confident person, or you're totally out of touch with yourself.

If your score is 9 or less, worry doesn't trouble you much.

If your score is between 10 and 18, you may often find yourself troubled by worry.

If you scored over 18, then worry could be a major source of pain in your life. You might want to talk about this with some trusted friends or one of your parents or a youth pastor.

The peace of Jesus is something way deeper than some self-help method to manage stress. It's a confidence that goes down to the core of your being—to your belly where rivers of living water can flow—that all things are in God's hands.

Before we go any further, we need to pause for one very important reminder: *Everybody* worries.

» Let Love Cast Out Fear

Paul said that when we live in the flow of the Spirit, God doesn't make us timid but gives us power and love. This isn't the only place in the Bible where we see a close connection between receiving love and living in power. The apostle John makes the same connection in one of the most famous statements in the Bible: *There is no fear in love . . . perfect love casts out fear.*

> There is no fear in love . . . perfect love casts out fear.

When we live in the flow of the Spirit, we let the perfect love of God wash over us until our fear starts to leave. Modern science has confirmed what John wrote so many centuries ago—*love and fear can't exist in our bodies at the same time.*

God wants to love you—and in loving you, to get rid of your fear.

Maybe it comes when you're alone with God. Maybe it happens when you pray with a few people. Maybe you find it when reading about the life of Jesus. Or it might come when you're singing a worship song or listening to music.

A lot of times the Spirit will use other people to help love cast out fear. Psychiatrist Edward Hallowell says it like this: *Never worry alone.* When worry grabs my mind, it attracts more worry. Worrisome thoughts reproduce faster than rabbits, so one of the most powerful ways to stop the spiral of worry is simply to tell my worry to a friend.

A while ago I had to speak in front of a large group of people. For some unknown reason, every time I thought about it, I started thinking about how I fainted twice when giving talks years ago. Soon I could feel the same tightness in my body, and I was afraid it might happen again. For a while I was so embarrassed about this fear that I kept silent. Finally I told a friend who said he'd pray for me. I felt such relief that I wondered why I hadn't told him sooner.

> * Never worry alone . . . one of the most powerful ways to stop the spiral of worry is simply to tell my worry to a friend.

In fact, when I gave the talk, I started by telling the whole audience about this fear. Now there were thousands of people with concerned expressions, worrying about me fainting during the talk. But I wasn't worried at all. I felt relieved that I didn't have to pretend I was okay. Just being reassured by another human being became a tool of the Spirit to get rid of my fear—because peace and fear are both contagious.

When Israel was to occupy the Promised Land, God gave them very interesting instructions: "Is anyone afraid or fainthearted? Let him go home so that the others will not become disheartened too." In an army, in a school, on a team, or in a ministry, negativity, fear, and discouragement are contagious. But courage is definitely contagious, too!

God's part in the process is that his peace, "which exceeds anything we can understand ... will guard your hearts and minds as you live in Christ Jesus." By this Paul doesn't mean just peace *from* God; he's talking about the peace that God *himself* has. *That* peace will guard our hearts and minds!

Have you ever flown in an airplane? If so, you've noticed that airport security employees carefully check every passenger in order to preserve peace and security.

Airports have resolved that they won't allow anyone who could threaten the well-being of a plane to board it, so they screen and remove anything that could be destructive. In the same way, every thought is like a passenger traveling in our brains. Each one has a little spiritual charge that's either positive or negative. Some help us deal with life: *God loves me. God is with me. God will guide me. I am never alone.* Some rob us of peace: *I can't handle this. I'm alone. I may not be adequate.*

The promise of God is that the Spirit will stand guard over our minds. It's not about us "trying harder." When I tell the Spirit my concerns, I'm "putting off worry." When I ask for the Spirit's help, I'm "putting on peace." And even though it takes effort when you first try it, over time it becomes a habit of your mind. That's why prayer is so important when it comes to getting rid of worry. Prayer is turning any concern over to God—as soon as we sense the concern. It's how we let the peace of God stand guard over our minds.

> God's peace, which exceeds anything we can understand . . . will guard your hearts and minds as you live in Christ Jesus.

» Take Direct Action to Face Your Fear

Living in peace doesn't involve only our inner thoughts; it also flows out of what we actually do.

Hearing messages about how God will take care of us isn't enough to remove our worry about our lives. If we're going to open up to the flow of the Spirit, we need to keep feeding our minds certain thoughts and information—but we also need to step out in trust.

I used to take my students to a summer camp with a ropes course 30 feet off the ground. It has several sections with colorful names such as "Jacob's Ladder" and "the Leap of Faith." The very last section is called "The Screamer." Want to guess why?

Before going on the ropes course, we all get a little lecture from the staff members who tell us how strong the harnesses are, how the ropes we're attached to could actually support tons of weight, and how the metal loops that clip everything together are practically indestructible. They explain to us that up on the ropes is a perfectly safe place to be. We have no reason to worry—and it's actually more dangerous to drive a car than to climb on this ropes course.

Everybody hears the same lecture. No one disagrees with the facts. We all nod our heads. We all believe what they say. But when we get up on the ropes, our stomachs don't agree with our minds. Jesus said, "Out of your bellies will flow rivers of living water," but that doesn't feel like what's flowing out of them the first time we're 30 feet off the ground.

The first time you go across the ropes, you're afraid. Thoughts flow automatically: *This is too high. This isn't safe. I'm gonna fall.* That flow of thoughts hasn't been changed by the lecture. Your mind hasn't been renewed. The second time up, you're probably still afraid ... but maybe a little less so.

But it's different when you look at the staff of the ropes course. They've been on the ropes hundreds of times—all summer long. And because they've put themselves through this experience time and again, their automatic thoughts have changed. Their stomachs have become convinced that up on the ropes is a perfectly safe place to be. Their minds have been renewed.

> Therefore, I urge you, brothers and sisters, in view of God's mercy, to offer your bodies as a living sacrifice, holy and pleasing to God — this is true worship. Do not conform to the pattern of this world, but be transformed by the renewing of your mind. (Romans 12:1–2)

The key moment during a ropes course comes when you're strapped in, ready to climb, and you say to your instructor, "On belay"—which I'm tempted to think is a French phrase meaning,

"I've lost my mind." Actually, to "belay" a rope means to make it absolutely secure, to fasten it to something immovable. It means now you're connected to something that will keep you from falling, and you will entrust your body to what you say you believe. You will walk by faith. On belay.

The instructor says, "Belay on."

You say, "Climbing."

Your instructor says, "Climb on."

And you're on your way.

You could listen to the lecture about the safety of the ropes a thousand times; you could even repeat the whole thing by memory—but that alone wouldn't take away the fear the first time you're on the ropes. But once you say "on belay" often enough, it's just a matter of time before your feelings start to change.

If you have only "information," it's not enough to bring about the transformation of the whole person. We can read book after book, listen to sermons, maybe even read the Bible, but we'll stay just as anxious as we were before. There's no way to get the peace of God from our heads to the rest of our bodies apart from just trusting God enough to directly tackle our greatest fears.

finding the flow in worry

≈ Reflect on a passage from the Bible, such as Psalm 23. Use your imagination to picture being shepherded by the Lord in green pastures beside still waters.

≈ Tell a friend before the worry gets a grip on your brain.

≈ Use a "breath prayer" such as, "God, I'm giving all my worries to you."

≈ Identify your fear and take one step to help you confront it.

≈ Get enough rest. "In peace I will lie down and sleep, for you alone, LORD, make me dwell in safety" (Psalm 4:8).

The Bible and prayer weren't given to us as ways to avoid anxiety. In the long run, any time we avoid doing the right thing out of fear, we die a little inside. But when we really place ourselves in the flow of the Spirit's peace is when we say "on belay" to God.

Let's say you're worried about a big project at school. Instead of procrastinating, you say "on belay." You give it your best effort with God's help. Each time your worry returns to your mind, you give that worry to God in prayer.

We go through this life one time. Some fantastic things will happen to us; some dreams will come true. Some really difficult things will happen to us, too; and those things will bring pain, problems, and disappointment. We can be sure of that. But whatever happens to us, we can go through this life worried—or we can go through it in peace.

Life is too short,
joy is too precious,
God is too good,
our soul is too valuable,
we matter too much
to throw away a single moment of our one and only life on worrying.
For the Spirit God gave us does not make us timid.

On belay.

PART FOUR

rescuing my time

Chapter 10

Let Your Talking Flow into Praying

When we're desperate, we call out for God. When we reach the end of our ropes, it's only human to reach out to God. When we're thrilled about something, we often thank God. When we're crushed by guilt, we cry out to God.

You pray more often than you know. Even in school we pray. People get concerned about legal issues with prayer in schools, but experience tells us that as long as there are tests in school, there will be prayer in school—even though it may be silent.

If someone were to ask, "How's your prayer life?" what would you tell that person? Is the status of your prayer life determined by how long you pray or how often? Is it measured by how many people you're praying for, or how much faith you're praying with, or how many of your prayers get answered?

If you believe in God, you've already started to pray—to enter into a conversation with God—because believing in God means believing God is always present, always listening to what you say. When you start to believe, you start to pray—because God's *always* right there with you. So let's look at the connection between prayer and "the rest of our lives."

» Is God in on Your Conversation?

It might be easier to understand prayer by viewing it like hanging out with a friend—and how being *with* that friend shapes what we say about him or her. For example, sometimes we speak *to* another person. Let's call that person Travis. Sometimes, though, we're talking to somebody else about Travis, but we're also speaking *in front of* Travis. So the fact that Travis is right there with us still influences the words we pick. Then there's a third scenario: We could talk about Travis *in his absence*, and now what we say about him might be quite different.

1. Speaking *to* someone.
2. Speaking *in front of* someone.
3. Speaking *in the absence of* someone.

True confession time: Have you ever spoken about someone when that person wasn't around and with words you wouldn't have used if that person were there with you? Author Mark Twain was once riding a train home from Maine after three weeks of really successful fishing—even though the state's fishing season was closed. He bragged about his huge-but-illegal catch to the only other passenger in the club car. The passenger grew increasingly gloomy during Twain's story. When Twain finally asked him who he was, the stranger mentioned that he was the state game warden (which means he was in charge of enforcing all wildlife laws).

"Who are you?" the warden asked.

"To tell the truth," Twain said, "I'm the biggest liar in the whole United States."

A lot of times when I'm speaking *to* someone or *in front of* someone, I hide my real heart. If I'm trying to make a good impression, experiencing a first date, or talking to someone in authority, I filter what I say. When I'm speaking to or in front of somebody — like maybe a teacher, a parent, or a coach — there's something going on in me that affects what I say because of that person's presence. There's always at least some effort that goes into this, even if we're not aware of it. And so I crave a place where I can go to be "my real self," where I don't feel I need to guard my words or body language to influence someone else's impressions of me.

Now let's bring God into the picture. The reality with God is that we're *never* speaking or acting *in God's absence.* The psalmist writes, "Where can I go from your Spirit? Where can I flee from your presence? If I go up to the heavens, you are there; if I make my bed in the depths, you are there." Yet God lets us sometimes feel as though we're away from him, and I believe God does that for a reason. Have you ever behaved differently at school when you knew the principal was standing in the hallway and looking in your direction? Why? It wasn't because your heart was changed. It wasn't because you saw that principal and thought, *Oh, I want to be a model citizen.* You behaved well because you didn't want to get in trouble!

You see, God doesn't want forced obedience. God is so huge that if God were "too visible," people would offer God forced obedience without really showing their hearts. So God makes it possible, because of his gigantic love for us, to live as if God weren't actually here.

This reality leads to some clashes in our spiritual lives. I went to a Christian college, and there was a long-running tradition to determine who would pray before meals — "the thumbs game," we called it. Everyone would raise their thumbs, and whoever raised their thumbs last was the one to pray. Then we'd all bow our heads, and that person would say, "Oh God, we love you so much, it's so good to pray to you!"

I didn't think about it at the time, but years later I thought, *You know, God must have been saying, "Hey, if it's so good to pray to me, then how come the loser of the thumbs game is always the one who has to do it?"*

When we played the thumbs game, it was as if we believed God wasn't watching. But then when we went to pray, we believed God suddenly tuned in. This is why people sometimes speak in one voice but pray in an entirely different voice — maybe a voice they believe sounds "holier" or something. We live with a kind of spiritual split personality.

> The goal of prayer is to live all of my life and speak all of my words in the joyful awareness of God's presence.

The goal of prayer isn't to get good at praying, as many people probably assume, or to set new records for how much time we spend praying. *The goal of prayer is to live all of my life and speak all of my words in the joyful awareness of God's presence.*

Prayer becomes real when we grasp the reality and goodness of God's constant presence with "the real me." Jesus lived his everyday life totally aware of his Father being right there with him. For example, when he went to raise Lazarus from the dead, Jesus began by "looking up to pray." In our day most people close their eyes when they pray. But for Jewish people in those days, praying with your eyes open was normal. It reminded them, *God is right here, right now, in my real world.*

> *"Father, I thank you that you have heard me. I knew that you always hear me, but I said this for the benefit of the people standing here, that they may believe that you sent me."*

Jesus knew God was listening to him not just when Jesus prayed, but all the time — whenever he spoke. God was always responding to Jesus' words, whether Jesus was talking to God or to someone else. For Jesus, there wasn't a huge difference between praying and just speaking. Sometimes when Jesus healed a person, he'd speak directly to the person he was healing. Sometimes he'd speak directly to God. It didn't really matter because he was always speaking in front of God, and God was always responding.

» Talk to God about Your Problems

Think about the major categories of your life: Your friendships, your family, school or work, your emotions, your habits, your moral decisions, your health, your physical appearance. Can you identify at least one problem in any of those categories?

If you can, then you have a fantastic trigger for prayer.

We get tricked into believing that we worry because we have problems and that "If we just didn't have problems, then we wouldn't worry anymore." The good news? *Our problems will go away*. The bad news? *They won't go away until the day we die*. You'll be amazed at how your problems stop bothering you when you're dead. Until then, though, life will be full of problems.

I've got to pray about what's in me, not what I wish were in me.

Today, try to see each of your problems as an invitation to prayer. Maybe you're mad at someone. Tell God! An amazing example of this is found in the life of Elisha. One day a huge gang of young guys started making fun of him. "Get out of here, baldy!" they told him. The Bible says Elisha turned toward them and called down judgment from heaven, and then 42 of them were mauled by two bears. It doesn't seem like the prayer of a spiritual giant, but Elisha prayed what was in him. Will God send a bear or two after someone you're mad at? Probably not, but you'll never know if you don't pray.

Either way, God will use your problems to grow a better you.

» Talk to God about What You Want

Sometimes I don't pray because my real thoughts seem unspiritual:

- I wonder if I'll make the team.
- I wonder if I'm putting on too much weight.
- I wonder if my friends think I'm interesting to be around.

So when I pray, I end up praying about things I think I *should* be concerned about: World peace, any sick relative, and global warming. But my mind keeps wandering toward stuff that I'm seriously concerned about. The way to let my talking flow into praying is this: *I've got to pray about what's in me, not what I wish were in me.*

Shel Silverstein wrote "Prayer of the Selfish Child":

Now I lay me down to sleep,
I pray the Lord my soul to keep,
And if I die before I wake,
I pray the Lord my toys to break.
So none of the other kids can use 'em . . .
Amen.

Little kids come to their parents with all kinds of requests: Awesome, foolish, generous, *and* selfish. What matters to parents, though, is that their children come to them. They know they can guide their kids' growth—as long as their kids speak openly with them. It's easier to help a heart that's selfish than a heart that's faking.

As long as we have unresolved problems, unfulfilled desires, and even a tiny bit of faith, we have all we need for a dynamic prayer life.

Chapter 11

Temptation: How *Not* to Get Hooked

Recently my wife and I went fly-fishing for the first time. Our guides told us, "To catch a fish, you have to think like a fish." They also said that to a fish, life is about maximum appetite fulfillment with minimum energy expense. To a fish, life is "See a fly, want a fly, eat a fly." A rainbow trout never reflects on where his life is headed. Fish are just a collection of appetites. A fish is a stomach, a mouth, and a pair of eyes.

While we were on the water, I was struck by how dumb fish are. *Hey, fish! Swallow this. It's not the real thing; it's just a lure. You think it'll feed you, but it won't. It'll trap you. If you were to look closely, fish, you'd see the hook. You'd know that once you're hooked, it's just a matter of time before your enemy reels you in.*

You'd think fish would wise up and notice the hook or see the line. You'd think fish would look around at all of their fish friends who go for a lure, fly out of the water, and never return. But they don't. It's crazy, really. We say fish swim together in a school, but they never learn.

Aren't you glad people are smarter?

Or are they?

Temptation is painful to us because when we give in, it doesn't hurt us from the outside; it hurts from the inside. Temptation tries to get our appetites to overrule our deepest values. Temptation strikes where we're most vulnerable, but life in the flow of the Spirit is about more than avoiding temptation. In fact, temptation also comes to us where we most need to grow. If I need patience, there will be some difficult people in my life to help me develop it. If I'm tempted by jealousy, then the person I'm jealous of can help me learn grace. Each temptation I face offers a step in the direction of the me I want to be.

But how can I keep Really Living when I'm tempted?

» Ask for Help

Nothing makes temptation more powerful than aloneness, but we don't face temptation alone. Paul writes, "No temptation has overtaken you except what is common to us all. And God is faithful; he will not let you be tempted beyond what you can bear. But when you are tempted, he will also provide a way out so that you can endure it." In Genesis 39 when Joseph was being chased around by a woman who wasn't his wife, this literally meant he was running out of the room.

But I believe the single most common "way out" involves talking with another person about our temptations. A friend of mine wrestles with gossip, but early on in our relationship he made one of the most honest confessions I've ever heard: "If you want to keep something top-secret, don't tell me—I leak!"

There was something so cool about his honesty. And instead of being pushed away, I was pulled toward him. We talked and prayed over why he was tripped up by gossip, where it got him in trouble, and how he could get free. He eventually became one of the friends to whom I entrusted my deepest secrets.

Ask, "Where Will This Lead?"

When I feel like walking down the wrong road, it starts by shutting down God's voice within me. I shut it down by not talking about this desire with wise friends who know what's best for me. I shut it down by not looking carefully at Bible verses on the subject and thinking about them. I shut it down by not thinking about what God would say about my situation. It's all related to Paul's warning about shutting down the Spirit within us: "Do not quench the Spirit," he writes. The word *quench* is similar to the word *extinguish*—as in fire extinguisher—which is something we never want to do when it comes to God's Spirit within us.

Anytime I have a want, the Spirit nudges me to set it before God and ask the question, "Lord, what do you want me to do with this?" Or I ask myself, *If I walk down this road, where will it lead in the long run—toward or away from the me I want to be?*

God's answer can always be trusted because God never leads us to handle desire in sinful ways.

Ask, "What Are My Deepest Values?"

The battle against temptation is a worthy fight; but if we try to hold back desire, it'll just wear us out. We've got to have a really clear picture of what kind of people we want to become and why. For instance, one day I wrote down all the reasons why I'd like to handle sexuality in an honorable way: What it might do to my wife if I didn't, how my children would be affected, what would happen to my work and ministry, and how it would feel to be haunted by guilt and failure.

Job put it this way: "I made a covenant with my eyes not to look lustfully at a girl." For instance, what if I'm at the beach and I see a female out of the corner of my eye? What if I tell myself that if I look over at her, then maybe I'll get a little jolt of sexual energy? Because of what Job said, my next thought is, *I don't have to look. I can* not *look!* The thought that follows is this: *Instead of feeling as though I'm missing out on a little thrill, by* not *looking at her, I'll have a power I didn't know I had. I can be free, and that freedom produced by the Spirit feels good.*

Real freedom isn't the external freedom to gratify every appetite; it's the internal freedom not to be locked up by our appetites.

Temptation promises that we can be free to fulfill our appetites as much as we want. See a fly, want a fly, eat a fly. Temptation promises freedom, but it actually makes us slaves. There's always a hook. Real freedom isn't the external freedom to gratify every appetite; it's the internal freedom not to be locked up by our appetites. We're more than just a stomach, a mouth, and a pair of eyes!

» Check Your Soul Satisfaction

When we're hungry, anything (and sometimes everything!) on the menu looks good. In the same way, when our souls are dissatisfied, sin starts to look really satisfying. That's why we have to pay attention to the level of soul satisfaction in our lives.

On the dashboard of any car are certain lights that tell us how hot the engine is running or when we're about to run out of gas. They're commonly called "idiot lights"—I suppose because only an idiot would ignore them. In the same way, the main light on the dashboard of our hearts is our "soul satisfaction light." That's why there are so many commandments in the Bible that point us to joy: "The joy of the LORD is your strength" and "Rejoice in the Lord always; again I will say, rejoice!"

Why do smart people keep getting hooked like those rainbow trout? What makes people with high IQs so vulnerable to temptation when it's obviously such a dumb step? We become vulnerable to temptation when we're dissatisfied with our lives. The deeper our dissatisfaction, the deeper our vulnerability ... because we were made for soul satisfaction. We can't live without it. If we don't find soul satisfaction in God, we'll look for it somewhere else. That's why Jesus begins the Sermon on the Mount not with rules about morality, but with good news that points right to the cravings of the soul: *Blessed.*

Blessed.

Blessed are *not* just the winners that society says are blessed. Blessed are *not* just the supermodels. Blessed are *not* just the glamorous and the popular who can attract glamorous and popular boyfriends or girlfriends.

Blessed are the troubled. Blessed are the "abnormal." Blessed are those who never got asked to the prom, who never got asked to dance.

Blessed, blessed, blessed. Blessed are you—not because you can have every desire fulfilled, but because you're way more than just a collection of your desires. Blessed are you because you're more than a stomach, a mouth, and a pair of eyes. Blessed are you because what you really ache for is to be loved by and connected to God, and now Jesus says that love, that life, that connection is yours if you want it—through him.

Do you want it?

» Don't Stay Down!

It's no accident that the devil is called the Tempter, but don't forget that he's also called the Accuser. As soon as Satan gets someone to give in to temptation, he'll take things further and attempt to convince that person that once you give in, you're beyond rescue. Not true!

The Spirit is just the opposite, always looking to "deliver us from evil." When we do give in, the flow of the Spirit moves us toward forgiveness, redemption, and healing.

I was running on a beach early one morning, discouraged because I wasn't seeing progress in my life. I felt like I was still wrestling with the same selfishness and fear that I had many years ago. Because it was so early, the beach was deserted. But then I saw a man walking toward me—a big old guy and bald as could be. He was wearing just a pair of long, floral swimming trunks, and his great big belly was hanging over the top of them. He looked like Santa Claus on summer vacation.

I intended to give him a casual nod of my head, but he was having none of that. He looked me right in the eye and stuck his right arm all the way out to the side, silently holding a huge hand in the air—he was insisting on a high-five! The man had *attitude*. So I smacked his hand with mine, and he gave me a nod of satisfaction. It was almost as if he were saying, "We're connected now. It's good that we're on this beach together. Great to have shared a moment with you."

Immediately I had a sense of being spoken to—and whether or not it was from God, only God knows: *I'm glad you're here. I'm not neutral about your existence. This is a little picture of grace. Don't be discouraged, not even about your own failings.*

To this day, every time I remember the man on the beach, I think about God.

Blessed.

Chapter 12
Know Your Primary Flow-Blocker

USA Today once ran a series of articles about the 10 most difficult things to do in sports. Number five was returning a professional tennis serve. Number four was hitting a golf ball long and straight (even though it's just sitting there on the tee). Number three was pole-vaulting higher than 15 feet. Number two was driving a race-car at megaspeed without dying. But the hardest feat in athletics? Hitting a professionally thrown baseball.

A few years ago a friend of mine named Ned Colletti, who was vice president of the San Francisco Giants baseball team at the time, asked if I'd speak at a chapel service. He offered to let me take batting practice with John Yandle, the batting-practice pitcher for Barry Bonds. I thought it would be a good chance to benchmark my athletic skills.

I never played organized baseball; but when I was a kid, we played on a vacant lot where the best pitcher around was Steve

Snail. In fifth grade I could hit his pitches better than anyone else in the neighborhood. (There was only one other kid in the neighborhood, and she was in first grade—but I was still the best.)

I did pretty well against Snail, I thought. *Let's see how this goes.*

At the batting cage in AT&T Park, John wound up and let go, and I heard the sound of the ball hitting the net behind me.

He's not just lobbing them in there, I thought. *He wants to see if I can hit his best stuff.*

John wound up again. The second pitch, the ball had already been in the net for several seconds by the time my bat got over the plate. So I kept starting my swing earlier until eventually I began my swing about the same time I saw him start his windup. I hit several foul balls and a few dribblers that might have gone fair. I was feeling pretty good.

Then he said, "Do you want me to put a little zip on one?"

And I realized those *had* been his lobs.

"Sure!" I said. "It's been hard to time these slow balls."

He wound up. I never saw it.

I asked him if that was his best pitch.

"No," he said, "you wouldn't want to see that."

"What level player would hit that well?" I asked.

"A good high school player would crush it," he said.

That day I learned there's a gigantic gap between sandlot baseball in my old neighborhood and major league talent in San Francisco. It's not just that I wasn't good—I didn't know enough to realize how "not good" I was.

But that doesn't happen just in sports. We can fool ourselves about our intelligence, for example. I may believe I'm pretty smart until I read about a kid who didn't miss a single question on the SAT, ACT, and PSAT combined. We fool ourselves about our talent, like when tone-deaf people sing karaoke at the top of their lungs and believe they're amazing. We fool ourselves about our appearance, like when a grandpa friend of mine boarded an airport tram and noticed a pretty young woman sitting nearby. She smiled at him, and he thought to himself, *I've still got it.* "Excuse me, sir," she said. "I can stand up. Would you like to take my seat?"

But one of the most common areas where people can end up fooling themselves is their spiritual lives. How many of us have given serious thought to how our lives would grade out—not by the standard of the neighborhood sandlot where we can always find a first-grader to outperform, but in the eyes of a holy, righteous, and truth-telling God? That's why the most dangerous force in the world isn't sickness or injury or pain.

It's sin.

Sin is a word that's not taken very seriously in our time. Neal Plantinga writes, "Nowadays, the accusation *you have sinned* is often said with a grin, and with a tone that signals an inside joke." *Sin* has become a word for hot vacation spots (Las Vegas is "Sin City") and dessert menus: Peanut Butter Binge and Chocolate Challenge are advertised as "sinful" pleasures.

But sin is the deadliest force because it takes us out of the flow of the Spirit. We must identify and understand this thing that threatens our ability to flourish, as only sin can keep us from becoming the people God wants us to become. All other challenges face us from the outside. Sin works its way inside, strangling our souls.

Your sin is closely connected to the passions and wiring God gave you. Sin doesn't look quite the same in anyone else. Like your fingerprints, your handwriting style, or your DNA, your sin pattern is unique to you.

» Signature Sins

We aren't tempted by stuff that disgusts us. Temptation rarely starts by trying to get us to do something 180 degrees in the opposite direction of our values. Temptation usually starts close to home with the passions and desires God wired into us and then tries to pull them a few degrees off course. That minor shift, if we let it happen, is enough to mess with the flow of the Spirit in our lives. So we need to learn to recognize the pattern of sins that are most tempting to us.

An author named Michael Mangis writes about what he calls "signature sin." It's based on the idea that my life has certain patterns, relationships, gifts, and things that are unique to me—yours does, too. My fingerprint is unique and could be recognized by an expert; my sin is kind of like that as well. Certain temptations are especially tough for me, and some sins are more attractive than others. Even if you and I both struggle with the sin of lashing out in anger, it'll probably get triggered and expressed in different ways for each of us. In other words, we don't sin at random. Our sin takes a predictable course. It's like my "sin profile."

Anyone who knows me well will probably be able to recognize my sin profile pretty quickly. In fact, other people sometimes know my sin profile better than I do.

In baseball, home-run hitters usually strike out a lot. It just goes with the territory. In the same way, the areas of our gifts and passions will also point toward our areas of vulnerability. Outgoing people who can inspire and encourage others can also be attracted to gossip. People who love to learn will be tempted to feel superior and talk down to others. People who are spontaneous and have a great appetite for life can struggle with impulse control. Optimistic types wander toward denial. Tell me your gifts, and I'll tell you your sins.

Mangis identifies nine of these patterns using an ancient system called the enneagram. It's a bit controversial because it's used by many different spiritual traditions, but it can be applied in a Christian framework.

These nine patterns are as follows:

Reformers have a deep love of perfection. They naturally have high standards of excellence, and their greatest fear is to be flawed. (They also make good surgeons and excellent golfers.) But they wrestle with perfectionism and self-righteousness. They're tempted to judge others whose standards aren't so high.

A friend of mine in Chicago, a surgical pathologist, fits this Reformer profile. He was charming and unmarried, but he cycled in and out of relationships because no one could ever quite measure up. I once asked him if he thought there was any connection between his inability to find a woman good enough to marry and his profession—cutting up dead tissue and putting it under a microscope to see what's wrong with it. Reformers call us to be our best selves—but they can also be hard to live up to.

Servers love to be needed. They're natural caregivers who fluff up your pillow even if it doesn't need fluffing. They remember birthdays and are the first ones up to do the dishes. Often Servers like positions where they support someone else, and they'll feel most comfortable in a social gathering when they have something to do.

While they're pulled toward helping out, their helping can sometimes come out of their *own* neediness. As a result they can sometimes drain other people with their need to lend a hand. Underneath their servanthood sometimes lurks low self-esteem that demands to be fed but can't seem to get filled up.

Achievers love to conquer challenges and perform in front of others. At their best they're motivated to grow, stretch, and learn. They can inspire and move people to action, and they often like to be in front of crowds. Giving a talk, which is the most common fear in America, often energizes them. If they don't have a chance to develop and shine, they lose motivation. Achievers want to make an impact on the world around them.

Their temptation is that they can live for their images, idolizing their own performances. If they're not careful, they'll be tempted to measure their successes by how much applause and recognition they get. When John the Baptist said that Jesus "must increase, but I must decrease," he described the kind of surrender that's most difficult for an achiever. Self-centered achievers can act like they're serving God, but they're really serving themselves.

Artists love beauty and have a strong desire to be unique. They love to express their individuality in bold ways. They often have a very keen sense of what kind of "look" they want to effect, or what life they want to create. Sometimes they can't even express it in words, but it comes out in their art or music or actions.

While they bring color and stylishness to a world that might otherwise be dull, their sensitivity can make them vulnerable to emotional swings, and their desire to be special can become their whole focus. Their temptation is connected to the need to be different. In their need to be special and stand out, they may look down on "ordinary people."

Thinkers like to "know"—and they like to know *everything.* At their best they're the investigators, scientists, and inventors among us. They love to discover truths that no one else has ever seen and master knowledge or skills or hobbies on their own. They often have amazing memories for the information they're interested in, and a lot of times they're quite introverted. If you're a thinker, you probably like your own space.

While thinkers love knowledge, knowledge can "puff them up." Sometimes thinkers love being right more than they love the people around them. Thinkers don't like to lose an argument, and they may even believe they've never actually lost one. They don't like to be interrupted, and many times they can be by themselves for hours, if not days. That doesn't mean they're more spiritual; they just have a low need to be around people. Thinkers aren't fun to argue with—unless you're one, too!

Loyalists were born to be team players. They crave causes they can give themselves to and communities they can believe in. At their best they help everyone else become better. They're usually pretty sharp and often speak well, although they may not always speak up. But they can grow pessimistic when they feel let down—which is bound to happen sometimes. They're tempted to push responsibility onto somebody else.

Loyalists' suspicion of God is that he's fickle, hard, or unfair; and their signature sin is fear. If Loyalists gets their feelings hurt, they can be tempted to withdraw or pout.

Enthusiasts are wired to be the life of the party. They can add zest and color to the lives of everyone around them; and in their perfect world, they'd be the bride at every wedding (and the corpse at every funeral). The Enthusiast often has a gift for storytelling—and they may talk about themselves a lot. If you talk with them about their problems, they may listen to you at first, but it just doesn't seem to stick with them.

Once while I was in a restaurant with a friend, every time we ordered something, the server said "superb" or "excellent choice" or "brilliant." We finally asked her, "Do you ever say, 'That was really stupid,' or 'That's going to taste terrible'?" The mask came off, and she said, "No. In the kitchen we actually have a list of affirmations, and every time somebody orders something, we have to give them one of those affirmations."

Enthusiasts don't need a list of affirmations because they're *always* saying "cool," "awesome," "wow," "fabulous," or "great." They can live for years without seeing the pain or darkness in other people or themselves. They're also tempted to make life become all about chasing after positive feelings—and they become miserable if they feel they're not getting enough attention.

Commanders are created to understand power and leadership, to know how it works and feel a natural pull toward it. If this is you, being strong is very important to you. You have a need to lead. Opposition actually energizes you. But power can become an end in itself, and you can get frustrated when you don't get your own way. Other people might be scared by you if they don't agree with you.

When we took our dog for obedience training, the instructor said, "When you're giving your dog an order, you must always be above your dog. Never get down and look your dog in the eye when you're giving him an order, because you must establish your dominance. If the dog wants to go outside and scratches at the door, you never respond to the dog and let him go out. You make the dog do a trick first, and then you let him go out the door."

If you're a commander, you don't like to be coached, taught, corrected, or led. And sometimes that can be a problem.

Peacemakers have a natural love for everybody getting along; they thrive when life is calm. Peacemakers love the verse, "How good and pleasant it is when God's people live together in unity!" Peacemakers can bring together families, schools, neighborhoods, and workplaces.

But peacemakers can be tempted to seek peace no matter how much it costs, using their relational skills to blend in and avoid any kind of conflict or risks because of their attachment to comfort. They often suffer from "incurable niceness" when courage is what's actually needed. A peacemaker friend of mine used to leave the table to empty the wastebasket anytime a conflict broke out at dinnertime.

REFORMER

Strengths: Internal standard of what's good, noble, and beautiful. Calls others to live better lives

Weaknesses: Can be prideful. Holds high standards that can lead to secret, inner sense of inadequacy

Example: The prophet Amos, who carried a plumb line to show Israel the standard God expected of society

SERVER

Strengths: Lives out love in action. Has a natural other-centeredness that makes people feel cared for

Weaknesses: Can use "giving" to manipulate others. Sometimes mistakes servanthood with fear or low esteem

Example: Martha, who was busy serving while her sister Mary sat at Jesus' feet

ACHIEVER

Strengths: Strong desire to grow. Ability to accomplish and add value to the lives and world around them

Weaknesses: Temptation to be preoccupied with one's own success. Sometimes uses other people to receive applause or approval

Example: Solomon, who sought achievement in education, finance, culture, and the arts

ARTIST

Strengths: Loves beauty and goodness. Brings imagination to life, love, and faith

Weaknesses: Finds that the need to be different can become an end in itself. Can be tempted to give in to impulses and live an undisciplined life

Example: King David, who had strong gifts as a poet, dancer, and composer of many psalms

THINKER

Strengths: A discoverer, inventor, and lover of logic. A passion for truth — even when it's costly

Weaknesses: Conviction of being right can lead to arrogance. Can be tempted to withdraw from relationships and love

Example: The apostle Paul, who loved to study, reason, explore, and teach

LOYALIST

Strengths: Faithful and dependable when the chips are down. Loves to be part of a great team

Weaknesses: Prone to skepticism or cynicism. When threatened can be pushed into isolation by fear

Example: Elisha, who became Elijah's steadfast companion and protégé

ENTHUSIAST

Strengths: High capacity for joy and emotional expression. Enthusiasm that can be contagious

Weaknesses: Needs to be the center of attention. Needs to avoid pain, which can lead to escape or addiction

Example: The apostle Peter, who was the first one to leap out of the boat — even if it meant sinking

COMMANDER

Strengths: Passion for justice and desire to champion great causes. Charisma to lead that inspires others

Weaknesses: Need for power that can cause others to feel used. Sometimes relies on fear and intimidation to get own way

Example: Nehemiah, who was moved to action—rallying followers and defying opponents—when he heard Jerusalem was in ruins

PEACEMAKER

Strengths: Natural ability to listen well and give wise counsel. Easy-going, low-maintenance relational style

Weaknesses: Tends to smooth things over and avoid conflict. Is passive

Example: Abraham, who was a peacemaker with his wife, his nephew Lot, and foreign leaders—even attempting to mediate between God and Sodom and Gomorrah.

- Which category best describes you?
- Tell a friend or two, and see if it matches their observations of you.
- What does this tell you about your sin pattern and temptation?

It's critical to learn the patterns at the core of the me you want to be, as well as the sin patterns that go along with them, because you're the most vulnerable when you're not self-aware. Jesus warned about people who go around taking the specks out of other people's eyes while not noticing the logs in their own eyes. My signature sin is my own log—so attractive to me that it's my biggest danger; so close to me that I may not even see it.

As I become more aware of my signature sin, I sometimes wish I could be like someone else. I fall into the Achiever category, so I sometimes believe I'd be less sinful if I were a Server. But every category wrestles with sin; they just do it in different ways. Knowing that every category has its own hidden temptations helps me be less likely to envy someone else when I'm doing badly. And it helps me not to judge someone else when I believe I'm doing well.

Finally, knowing other people's patterns helps us live in community better. As we learn about others' patterns, we get more patient with people whose signature sins are different than ours. We can make sure Servers don't always get stuck in "serving" mode; we can encourage Peacemakers to speak honestly when they get frustrated.

When we know ourselves and each other better—and when we walk in love—we can be the best version of ourselves: God's hand-signed version of ourselves.

That's the signature we really want.

Chapter 13

When You're Out of the Flow, Jump Back In

There's only one pair of eyes that you can never look directly into: Your own. There are parts of yourself you'll never see without a mirror, camera, or outside help.

It's the same way with your soul.

In one sense you know yourself better than anyone in the world. You're the only one who knows your inner thoughts, feelings, and judgments. In another way you know yourself *worse* than anyone else can know you because we all make excuses, justify, minimize, forget, and exaggerate—and we often don't even know when we're doing it.

There is a me I cannot see.

Carol Tavris and Elliot Aronson have written a wonderfully disturbing book called *Mistakes Were Made (But Not by Me)*. This book describes the mental tricks we play to deceive ourselves. For example, most faculty members rate themselves as above-average teachers, and almost all high school students rate themselves as above average in social skills. Most people who are admitted to hospitals due to car crashes that *they* caused rate themselves as above-average drivers. Even when people have this particular concept explained to them, most rate themselves as above average in their ability to handle this concept!

When I see bad behavior in you, I assume it's because of your faulty character. When it happens in me, I explain that it's because of extraordinarily tough circumstances. When your parents yell at you, you're likely to say they have an anger problem. But when you yell at your parents, you're apt to excuse it, saying they just don't understand you.

We're also guilty of what's called "confirmation bias." In other words, we pay attention to experts who agree with the opinions we already agree with, but we ignore or minimize evidence that disagrees with our opinions.

Our memories aren't just faulty; they're faulty in ways that agree with our egos. People remember voting during elections in which they didn't vote and giving money to charities they never gave to. They remember getting better grades than they did. The book *Egonomics* tells of a survey where 83 percent of the people were confident in their own abilities to make good decisions, but only 27 percent were confident in the decision-making abilities of the people they worked closely with.

We all view ourselves in crazy, image-distorting fun house mirrors. People who know me well can always see these things in me more easily than I see them in myself. This is why we're often shocked when someone sees past our defenses and into our souls. It's not that they're geniuses. It's just that I'm sitting right in my blind spot.

» Acknowledge Your Own Blind Spot

Without the flow of the Holy Spirit, we can't even see our sin. Here's a vivid picture of how this works. When we lived in

Chicago, there was a season when we'd often get heavy snow. (It started in August and ended in June. At least it seemed like it.) To melt snow and ice, the street crews cover the roads with rock salt, which ends up covering the vehicles' windshields. At night, driving by headlights in the dark, you don't know the film is there. But then the sun comes up. And since sunlight is 500,000 times more intense than moonlight, the sunlight shows all the salt on the windshield—and suddenly you can't see out of it. You can't go anywhere. You have two choices: Get the windshield cleaned or drive only at night. Avoid the light.

> This is the verdict: Light has come into the world, but people loved darkness instead of light. (John 3:19)

» Invite the Spirit to Examine Your Soul

Trying to see the truth about myself is like trying to see the inside of my own eyeballs. "Who can discern their own errors? Forgive my hidden faults," the psalmist wrote. Fortunately, we aren't left on our own. The Spirit is already at work in us. Our job is simply to listen and respond.

Once, in the middle of the night, Nancy and I were lying in bed when we heard a tremendously loud beeping sound. Nancy gave me an elbow to the ribs: "What is that sound?"

I knew that if I acknowledged hearing the sound, it'd be my job to check it out. So I said, "What sound?" But I had to say it very loudly so she'd hear me over the tremendously loud beeping sound.

And she said, "That tremendously loud beeping sound."

"Oh, *that* sound! Let me go find out."

I went into the hallway, found the problem, and took care of it. When I got back to bed, Nancy asked, "What was it?"

I told her it was the smoke detector.

"What made it stop?"

I told her I took the battery out.

"You can't do that," she said. "There could be a fire in the house somewhere."

"Nancy," I explained patiently, "we're upstairs. There's no smoke, we can't smell anything, there's no heat coming from anyplace. I checked. Do you smell any smoke? I don't smell any smoke. It was clearly a battery problem. Trust me. I took care of it."

We went back to sleep.

The next morning I had an early breakfast meeting, so while everyone else in the family was still sleeping, I went downstairs to leave the house. As I did, I noticed some odd malfunctions: The hall lights downstairs didn't work. The garage door wouldn't open automatically. It was strange, but I didn't think much more about it. Then 40 minutes into my breakfast meeting, the server came up to verify who I was and then delivered a message.

"Your wife called," she said. "She asked you to come home. She said the house is on fire."

I went home. Fire trucks were parked all over the cul-de-sac. I watched the outside of our white house turning brown and great clouds of smoke escaping into the neighborhood.

It turns out that a few delinquent birds had built their nest inside the chimney. It eventually started smoldering and set off that loud beeping sound. Because we didn't do anything (and when I say "we," it's my way of saying that mistakes were made, but not by me), a fire started behind the wall and did unbelievable damage.

All from a little bird's nest.

A stupid little bird's nest.

What kind of an idiot would take the batteries out of a smoke detector so he could sleep better during a fire?

That would be me.

The smoke detector wasn't my enemy; the fire was my enemy. The smoke detector was simply trying to help me.

Do you hear any beeping sounds in your soul?

Beeping can sound like this: You're having trouble with friendships. The people you used to hang out with seem more distant, and you feel misunderstood. But instead of looking closely at your relationships — instead of talking directly about them with others—you communicate mostly by texting and bury yourself in homework, hobbies, or TV.

Or you feel a twinge of pain during a documentary about famine in Africa. You vaguely wonder about how little money you give to help anyone. But you don't like how uncomfortable that feels, so you distract yourself by surfing the Internet.

Or you blow up at the people you're closest to. Your "beeping sound" is loneliness. And then you take the batteries out of the smoke detector by shutting yourself in your room and playing a few more video games, convincing yourself that your family members are all difficult people.

Sin, which blocks off life, is my enemy. The Spirit will often bring a sense of conviction about your sin. And when the Spirit does this, the best response isn't to smother the guilt but to get out of bed, take a look around the house, and put out the fire before it does more damage.

» Don't Get Used to the Beeping

One of the most heartbreaking statements in the Bible is about Samson, whom God created to be a man of great strength and power. After a lifetime of disobedience, Samson had pushed God out of his life. Then at a great moment of crisis, Samson stood up to use his God-given strength, but we're told, "He did not know that the LORD had left him." He'd lost all sensitivity to God's presence in his life.

God will help us find the truth about our souls if we're patient and open and willing. The psalmist asks God to do a kind of fearless searching because only God can give enough grace, strength, and truth to overcome our distorted vision. Left on my own, I'll rationalize or excuse or defend myself, calling "evil good and good evil," as Isaiah writes. But it's possible to allow our thoughts and responses to be guided by the Spirit.

One of the most important metaphors the Bible uses for sin is that of clothing. It speaks of "putting off" anger, slander, rage, greed, sexual impurity, and so on. And then it speaks of "putting on" those characteristics that flow from life in the Spirit. One of the ways you can think about sin is to use the acronym R.A.G.S. By and large those characteristics we're to "put off" will fit into one of these four categories:

R.A.G.S.

Resentment — mismanaged anger and bitterness

Anxiety — an inability or refusal to trust God; sins of passivity and timidity

Greed — mismanaged desire of all kinds

Superiority — self-righteousness and contempt for others

To make it concrete, you can grade yourself with an A, B, or C response:

"A" means things are going well.
"B" means there isn't much change either way.
"C" means I should probably pay attention to this.

Let the Spirit prompt you as you walk through this.

Resentment

≈ What's your irritability these days?
≈ Are you becoming less and less easily irritated?
≈ Do you attack or withdraw from others?
≈ Is your handling of anger getting better, getting worse, or in neutral?

Stop for a minute. Does the Spirit bring to mind anybody you need to patch things up with? Seek to set things right.

Anxiety

≈ What's the discouragement level in your life these days?
≈ Are you more frequently allowing concerns to cause you to pray?

≈ Do you have more or fewer fears these days about school, or friends, or what other people think of you?
≈ Do you allow your fears to keep you from doing what God wants?

Greed

≈ Is your self-control going up, down, or in neutral?
≈ Are you living with more openness and less hiddenness than you used to, living more of your life in the light?
≈ Do you find that what you desire and enjoy is increasingly in line with what God wants for you?

Superiority

≈ Are you becoming less selfish these days?
≈ How often during conversations do you comment on the positive traits in others instead of calling attention to yourself?
≈ Are you spending more or less time serving?

How much clarity did you have? Often we have to grow before God can show us deeper and more subtle layers of sin. Where did you find yourself with a "B" or "C"? Are there any particular behaviors you need to apologize for or clean up? Find a close friend and talk with him or her about what you're learning.

» Recognize the "Ministry of Conviction"

Jesus said that when the Holy Spirit came, the Spirit would *convict* people of sin. But conviction isn't the same thing as "getting caught."

After we moved from California to Illinois, I was driving home from preaching—a short mile and a half in the car—and I got pulled over.

"Do you know why I pulled you over?" the officer asked.

I hate that question.

"You came to a stop sign, but you didn't come to a complete stop. You just came to a roll. I noticed that your license plates are from out of state. In California they may be fine with it if you slow down to a roll at a stop sign. But you're in Illinois now, and in Illinois stop means *stop*."

I told him I was sorry, that I was distracted because I was coming home from church—did I mention I work at a church? Did I mention I work for God?

He told me he'd let me go if I'd say a Mass for him.

Sometimes people get caught doing something wrong, and then they feel pain. But pain isn't necessarily conviction over sin. It may just be embarrassment or frustration over being caught.

Conviction isn't the same thing as fear of punishment. Conviction is when I get a glimpse of what I'm capable of, as in, *How did I become the kind of guy who can do that? How did I become the kind of person who cheats on tests? How did I become the kind of person who tells lies to get what I want? How did I become the kind of person who's so gutless about what I say?*

When God is at work in me, though, the pain isn't about other people knowing or about consequences. That's all external. The pain of conviction is internal—it's over who *I am*. I respond by asking, *God, please send as much light as I can stand. Clean off the windshield of what I cannot clean.*

Clean me up.

» The Crucial Hope

When we turn from our sin, it's always done in hope. Guilt may be an important stop on the journey, but it's never supposed to be the end of the line.

Turning from sin is a gift God gives us for our own sake, not his. It doesn't increase God's desire to be with us. It increases our ability to be with God.

Ever see an animal turn from sin?

We have a dog and a cat. Our dog sleeps in a little house every night, and he always gets a treat before he goes to sleep. He expects it. He feels like he deserves it. When I stand up after 9 p.m., he goes crazy with anticipation. He stands at the door of the closet where the treats are, and he won't go into his house without a treat.

But sometimes the dog does a "bad thing," if you know what I mean. When that happens, and when we find the "bad thing," he doesn't expect a treat. He runs from us. He'll actually run into his house all by himself without a treat. He knows he's been bad.

(Sometimes our cat does bad things, too. But do you think the cat repents? No. Do you know why? Cats are evil. Somebody once said the difference between a cat and a dog is that a dog has a master, while a cat has employees.)

We often believe we need to turn from sin because God is mad at us and needs some time to cool off. We think of turning from sin as a way of punishing ourselves so maybe God will be less harsh with us. Not so.

Turning from sin is always done in the awesome promise of forgiveness.

» Can We Really Expect to Change?

Sometimes people are afraid that if they don't change fast enough, God will get irritated with them. They don't usually use these words, but they wonder, *How much sin can there be in my life before I need to start worrying? Is there a level of sin that's "acceptable" for a Christian? And if you go higher than that, you're in danger—like the number of concussions a football player can get before he should worry about his brain? Is it possible to be a Christian and just never grow?*

The issue isn't whether God will get tired of forgiving our sins. Forgiving is always the right response when someone sincerely turns from a sin. God isn't worried he might get taken advantage of. God's not afraid that some bad boy will use his charm to fool heaven.

The danger isn't that God won't respond to our sincere turning from sin; the danger is that we might become so tangled in the messed-up thoughts that sin produces that we'll become unable to turn from them.

This is the reason that sin must be taken so seriously. Paul told the church at Galatia, "Brothers and sisters, if someone is caught in a sin, you who live by the Spirit should restore that person gently. But watch yourselves, or you also may be tempted."

When the Spirit is helping us, we don't turn to that person in a judgmental way because we're never in a position to judge the amount of spiritual growth that's taken place in somebody else. Missionary Frank Laubach preached the gospel to a tribe that had a long history of violence. The chief was so moved by Laubach's presentation that he accepted Christ on the spot. He then turned to Laubach in gratitude and said, "This is wonderful! Who do you want me to kill for you?" That was the chief's starting point.

Only God knows what everyone's starting point is.

» Cling to a Bigger Hope

The bigger hope I cling to in the face of sin is not my goodness, but God's.

This year we had a daughter graduate from Azusa Pacific University. My wife spoke at the commencement ceremony, so we had a little gathering with a group of 50 or so faculty, alumni, and administrators before the ceremony. A few dozen people had graduated 50 years earlier, and they were also there to celebrate with these brand-new graduates.

At one point Jon Wallace, the university president, pulled three seniors into the center of the room and told us they were going to be serving under-resourced people in poor areas for several years after graduation. The graduating seniors said a few words about where they were going and why, and we applauded. They thought that was why they were there. Then Jon turned his back to the rest of us, faced the three students, and told them the real reason they were in the room.

"Somebody you don't know has heard what you're doing," Jon said. "He wants you to be able to serve the people where you're going without any obstacles. So he's given a gift. He's asked to remain anonymous, but here's what he's done for you."

Jon turned to the first student, who still owed a whole bunch of tuition money to the school, looked her in the eye, and said, "You've been forgiven your school debt of $105,000."

It took a few moments for the words to sink in. The student shook her head at first. The thought registered. She began to cry at the absolute unexpected generosity of a mountain of debt being wiped out in a moment by someone she'd never met.

Jon turned to the next student, who also owed the university money. "You've been forgiven your debt of $70,000."

Then Jon turned to the third student. By this time she knew what was coming. But it was as if she couldn't believe it was happening until she heard the words: "You've been forgiven your debt of $130,000."

All three students were trembling. Their lives had been changed in an instant by the super-generous heart of someone they'd never met. All of us who watched this exchange were so moved — it was as if we'd experienced the forgiveness ourselves. There wasn't a dry eye in the room. (And I wanted so badly to say, "I have a daughter who's graduating this weekend ...")

An unpayable debt. An unseen giver. An unforgettable gift. And the freedom of the debtors becomes a blessing to the world.

Grace.

The joy of forgiveness.

There is a bigger debt that we all share. We give it labels like *regret*, *guilt*, *shame*, or *brokenness* — sin. But God forgives us through Christ's sacrifice on the cross. We know what's coming, yet we need to hear the words just the same: Forgiven. Forgiven.

Forgiven.

PART FIVE

deepening my relationships

Chapter 14

Try Going Off the Deep End with God

Researchers once surveyed people about their favorite room in the house, and the top answer was the kitchen. People love that room. The top answer for teenagers was their bedrooms—places to chill out alone, away from the craziness the world can bring. Want to guess what the top answer was for mothers of young children?

The bathroom.

Why? It may be the only place where they can be out of the grasp of their little rug rats for at least a couple of minutes (assuming the door is locked). The idea is that they find someplace where they can be alone ... free from stress. They find "sanctuary"—a holy place.

God wants to give us sanctuary. It's awesome when a gathering of people can experience the presence of God, but there's a unique way that we experience the presence of God when we're alone.

Sometimes we're supposed to pray privately. It's good to pray with people; but when I'm praying and other people are listening, the fact that I know they're listening changes how I pray. Being alone with God, however, I can fully be myself.

In Jesus' day, almost no homes had private bedrooms. The "room" he's referring to when he says, "When you pray, go into your room, close the door and pray to your Father," might be a supply room where they kept feed and tools or a few small animals. That would be the only place where there might be a door. It would be the most humble room in a humble home.

Being alone with God . . . I can fully be myself.

> "When you pray, go into your room, close the door and pray to your Father, who is unseen. Then your Father, who sees what is done in secret, will reward you." (Matthew 6:6)

What's *your* "room"?

» Private Prayer Is Your Soul Alone with God

Jesus prayed. We're told that when Jesus was baptized, "as he was praying, the heavens opened," and the Spirit came upon him. The flow of the Spirit is closely connected to prayer, and after Jesus was baptized, he immediately went into 40 days of fasting and prayer.

Jesus prayed *when his life was crowded and draining.* After he began his public ministry, privacy became difficult. "The news about him spread all the more, so that crowds of people came to hear him and to be healed ... But Jesus often withdrew to lonely places and prayed."

Jesus prayed *when he faced important choices.* When it was time to choose his closest friends, he asked God for guidance. "One of those days Jesus went out to a mountainside to pray, and spent the night praying to God. When morning came, he called his disciples to him and chose twelve of them, whom he also designated apostles."

Jesus prayed *when he was sad or scared.* During Jesus' ministry his cousin, John the Baptist, was arrested and eventually executed. "When Jesus heard what had happened, he withdrew ... privately to a solitary place" to be alone with his Father.

Jesus prayed *when he needed strength.* One morning, "while it was still dark, Jesus got up, left the house and went off to a solitary place, where he prayed." When Simon Peter came looking for him, Jesus said, "Let us go somewhere else—to the nearby villages—so I can preach there also. That is why I have come."

Jesus prayed *when he was worried about people he loved.* When he was about to die, Jesus knew his disciples would fail. He told Simon Peter, "Satan has asked to sift all of you as wheat. But I have prayed for you, Simon, that your faith may not fail. And when you have turned back, strengthen your brothers."

Jesus prayed *when he faced a devastating problem.* "Jesus went out as usual to the Mount of Olives, and his disciples followed him. On reaching the place, he said to them, 'Pray that you will not fall into temptation.'" Then "he withdrew about a stone's throw beyond them, knelt down and prayed, 'Father, if you are willing, take this cup from me; yet not my will, but yours be done.'"

When Jesus prayed, things happened. One time he took Peter, James, and John to a mountaintop to pray, and "as he was praying, the appearance of his face changed, and his clothes became as bright as a flash of lightning."

A lot of times I find myself feeling guilty when I read those descriptions of Jesus in prayer—knowing I'm so far from his example. But I don't believe guilt helps us pray much more over the long haul. So think about this question: Do you think Jesus prayed a lot because he *wanted* to pray or because he thought he *should* pray? The answer might surprise you.

If you ever feel guilty about your praying, know that someone who's better at it than you are is already at work. Scripture says, "God's Spirit is right alongside helping us along. If we don't know how or what to pray, it doesn't matter. He does our praying in and for us, making prayer out of our wordless sighs, our aching groans. He knows us far better than we know ourselves ... and keeps us present before God."

I believe Jesus *wanted* to pray. And for us to pray much, or deeply, we need to change from what we think we *should* do to what we *want* to do. But that won't happen if we simply tell ourselves that we have to pray more. So let's not think about "shoulds" for a minute. How can we start to pray in a way that could actually help us *want* to pray?

Almost 20 years ago, I felt frustrated at my own lack of prayer. So I found a kind of prayer coach who advised me to spend a few moments after I prayed just jotting down what had gone on while I was praying. The single most frequent observation for me was that while I was praying, I was aware of being very tired.

"Did you tell the Lord about this?" my coach asked.

"No."

"Do you think it would be a good idea to talk to him about this?"

"Yes."

I began to learn that although I was trying to set aside time to pray, I had a hard time being *fully present*. We all know what it's like to be with another person when his or her mind is a million miles away. But I began to think that's how God felt when I was praying. After a period of frustration, my prayer coach suggested that I go outside alone and simply invite Jesus to come with me.

The next day I went to the ocean, took my shoes off, started to run, and invited Jesus to come along. And I discovered the strangest thing: When I thought I was *supposed* to be talking to Jesus, it felt really difficult; but now that all I had to do was *invite* Jesus, I couldn't stop thinking about him. My mind kept thinking about his being with me. I found myself wanting to point out the pelicans and the waves to him. People and concerns would pop into my mind, and I'd find myself telling Jesus about them.

Everything changed.

» Use Your Body in Prayer

Body language is an important part of communication, and we can use our bodies in lots of ways to help us pray. I mentioned earlier that in Bible times people generally prayed with their eyes open. A friend of mine who knows church history said people closing their eyes and bowing their heads to pray didn't become common until the 1800s—and then it was mostly to get children to settle down in Sunday school. There are records in Scripture of people praying as they stand, kneel, lie down on the ground, sit, stretch out their hands, lift their faces toward the sky, or bow them toward earth.

You are free to use your body and posture to help you turn your mind and heart to God:

- ≈ In confession I often have my head bowed, and I'll kneel; it helps me remember to be humble in that moment.
- ≈ In worship you might want to turn your face toward the sky.
- ≈ When I ask for guidance from God, I'll sometimes place my palms upward as a way of expressing with my body "whatever you want . . ."
- ≈ To honor God, I'll often sing worship music as a prayer.

» When Your Mind Wanders — The Spirit Is There, Too

Does your mind ever wander when you pray? Sometimes it's good to take a few deep breaths at the beginning of a prayer to slow down our brains and help us focus. But I've also figured out that sometimes my wandering thoughts can actually guide me into prayer.

I start praying, and then I imagine myself being wildly successful at something. Or I replay a conversation with a person who made me angry. Or I try to figure out how to solve a problem that worries me.

I used to think of those kinds of thoughts as blockers to prayer, but now I've started to think of them as prayers waiting to be prayed. Maybe the reason they pop into my mind isn't just because of my short attention span, but because they're actually what my mind is really concerned about. Instead of trying to push back these thoughts, it's better to talk to God about them. And then *bam*! I'm back in the flow of prayer.

» Let God's Face Shine on You

Have you ever heard that phrase "let God's face shine on you" before? Maybe you've heard it at the end of a church service? Ever wonder what it means? God gives us an amazing picture of what can happen in prayer when we watch a parent and a little kid interact. Imagine a one year old who looks at you and then just stares at you. You're charmed. He looks shyly at first, tilting his head away and looking out of the corner of his eye. You do the same. It's fun. Now he turns his face to look directly at you. You mirror what he does. There's a sudden noise behind him, and he looks startled—and you mirror his surprised look. He's so startled that he's about to cry, so you shift into a smile. He does the same, and he starts to giggle.

It seems like just a game, but it's actually more than that. When a little kid makes eye contact in this way, it's as though a connection is formed between the two of you. By playing the face game, you're actually giving the child peace. Because of that, he wants to play. No one has to tell children they "should" play. Children are wired for it. They love it.

In the Old Testament, God told Moses to give the Israelites this blessing: "The LORD bless you and keep you; the LORD make his face to shine upon you ... the LORD lift up his countenance upon you, and give you peace."

Is this what happened when Jesus prayed?

Prayer wasn't an energy-drainer for Jesus; it was an energy-giver. So it can be for us if we come to see God's face shining on us.

When someone cuts me down and wants to argue with me, I lose energy. When I talk with my best friend, I gain energy. God wants to talk with us as our friend.

> God's Spirit touches our spirits and confirms who we really are. We know who he is, and we know who we are: Father and children. (Romans 8:16 *The Message*)

Prayer, more than any other single activity, is what places us in the flow of the Spirit. When we pray, people get guidance, hearts get encouraged, sin gets confessed, believers get united, stubbornness gets melted, pride gets surrendered, evil gets defeated, illness gets healed, sadness gets comforted, faith is born, hope is grown, and love wins.

In prayer—in the presence of God—we come closest to being fully ourselves.

Chapter 15

Make Sure Your Relationships Are Life-Giving

More than anything else, people shape us. Some naturally help me live in the flow of the Spirit and make me want to be the best version of myself. They see the best of me when I cannot see it. They cheer me on when I grow toward it. They get in my face when I move away from it. They encourage me when I'm tempted to give up.

Plus, I like them.

» The Power of Connecting

What happens between you and another person is never *just* human-to-human interaction — the Spirit really wants to supercharge every one of your personal encounters. Some writers of Scripture talk about "the fellowship of the Spirit." *Fellowship* has become a churchy word that can make us think of basements and red punch and awkward conversation. But it's really a word for the flow of rivers of living water between one person and another, and we cannot live without it.

An academic publication called *The Journal of Happiness Studies* notes research about what makes humans Really Live. When researchers look at what makes really happy people different from less happy people, one factor consistently separates those two groups. It's not how much money you have; it's not your health, grades, attractiveness, IQ, or athletic success. It's the presence of loving, deep, laughter-producing, life-changing, meaningful relationships.

Spending meaningful time with people who care about us is vital to Really Living.

> Connectedness is not the same thing as knowing many people. People may have many contacts in many networks, but they may not have any friends.

Part of what it means to be made in God's image is our ability to connect with people, because God created human beings and then said, "It isn't good for man to be alone." Paul describes that connectedness in his letter to the Ephesians, saying they're "being rooted and established in love."

When a tree puts roots into the ground, those roots are able to take in nutrients and water; and the tree grows and has life and strength—but *only* if it's rooted. In the same way, we're rooted and our souls are fed by the love of God and other people. We experience this both physically and emotionally when we connect with others.

You're walking down the hallway, and someone you know smiles at you. They care about you through words, through listening, through prayer together. Whenever there's an exchange of real caring, it's as if the roots of your soul are getting fed. Every life has to have that kind of connecting.

How necessary is it? British scientist Donald Winnicott found that little kids who play near their mothers are more creative than children playing at a distance from them. Winnicott found that little kids are naturally more curious and adventurous in what might be called the "circle of connectedness." When they're within this circle, they take more risks. They show more energy. If they fall down, they're more likely to get back up. They laugh more than kids outside the circle.

Why? It's not as though the mom is doing something for the kid that the kid couldn't do for himself. She's not solving problems for this child or telling him how he ought to play. Instead, because love is present, that kid feels safe and cared for in her presence. He gets a little stronger. He gets bolder and more creative. Love frees up life in that child that would otherwise stay hidden.

When you're loved, it's not just that you get more from someone else—you also become more yourself. *You-ier.* Love brings the power to become the me I want to be. Loving people are literally life-givers. That's connectedness.

As children grow older and more capable, the circle gets bigger. At a year old, maybe they want to be within a few inches of their moms. When they're two, they can be several feet away but still in the circle. When they're three, the circle may be as big as a house.

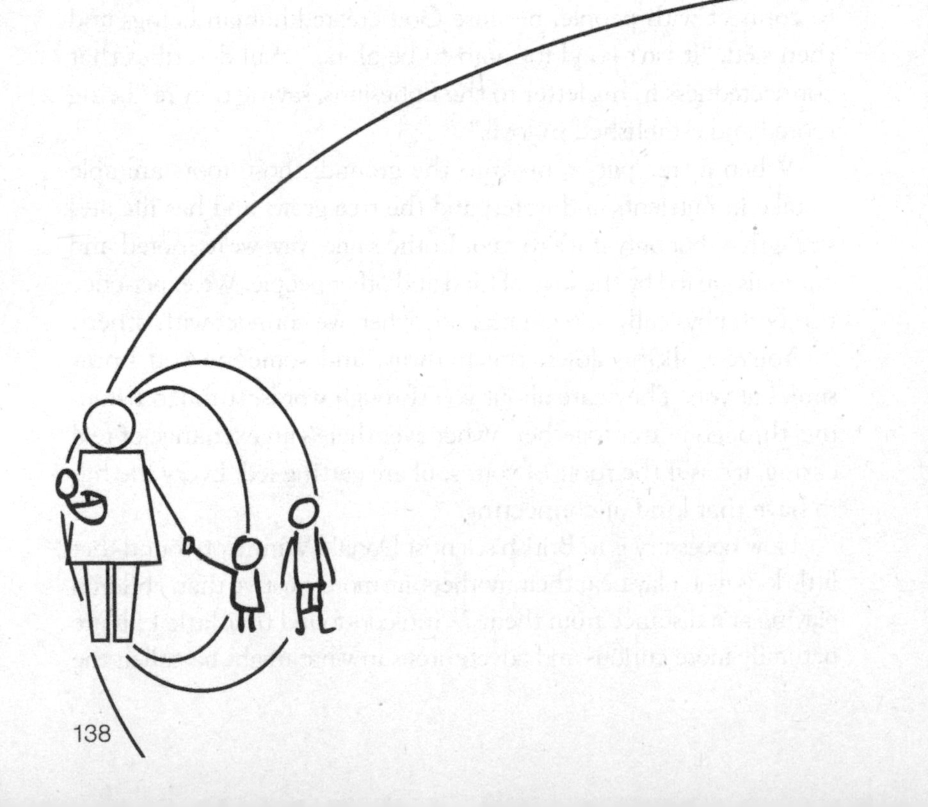

How about when they're 15—how far away do they want to be then? The circle is now the size of the solar system. They want to be tracing the orbit of Halley's Comet.

We Really Live when we're connected with God and people, and we get weaker when we're disconnected. Isolated people are more at risk for depression, anxiety, loneliness, low self-esteem, substance abuse, sexual addiction, and difficulties with eating and sleeping.

Physically, isolation can be powerful and destructive. Even animals that are isolated experience more physical problems than animals that aren't isolated. A friend of mine used to have a dog and a cat, and the dog and the cat fought for 10 years. Then one day the cat died, and you'd think the dog would have been happy. But he wasn't. He didn't want to eat. Day after day the dog wouldn't eat, until six weeks later the dog died. That's the power of connection.

People who are socially disconnected are between two and five times more likely to die from any cause than those who have close ties to family, friends, and other relationships. And believe it or not, those with bad health habits (such as cigarette smoking, overeating, and physical inactivity) who still remain connected live *longer* than disconnected people with great health habits.

The disciple John says, "Anyone who does not love remains in death." When we live in isolation, we're more likely to give in to temptation or discouragement. We're more likely to become selfish. Not only do *we* suffer when we live in disconnectedness, but others whom God has placed around us also get cheated out of the love God intended to give them through us.

> Loners who care only for themselves spit on the common good. (Proverbs 18:1 *The Message*)

We were designed to Really Live in connectedness. This doesn't mean we have to become more outgoing. Some of the shyest people I know have some of the deepest friendships. However, Really Living in connectedness *does* mean that we'll have to learn to identify the life-giving people around us—and figure out how to give the power of connectedness to others so we can grow those relationships.

So let's open the boxes and look at the gifts that connectedness brings.

» The Gift of Delighting

Love is mostly something you do, not something you feel. The circle of connection is marked by servanthood. "You, my brothers and sisters," Paul says, "were called to be free. But do not use your freedom to indulge the sinful nature; rather, serve one another humbly in love"—because what marks God's kingdom is when people serve one another.

A son remembers his mom's birthday and writes her a note telling her how grateful he is for her. A friend mentions a video game he's interested in, and his friend remembers and finds a copy to give him. (Why? Just because.) A young guy notices an elderly neighbor's lawn that needs cleaning up, and he gathers some buddies to do it—for free. People in a small group Facebook each other all through the week as a way to express their care.

A wise man once said that just as the three laws of real estate are "location, location, location," the three laws of relationship are "observation, observation, observation." People who give life to us are people who actually notice us. They know what we love and fear. When we work to truly notice someone else, love for that person grows in us. When we work to really notice someone else, our own souls Really Live.

If you can't do great things, Mother Teresa used to say, do little things with great love. If you can't do them with great love, do them with a little love. If you can't do them with a little love, do them anyway.

Love grows when people serve.

» The Gift of Commitment

One of the marks of the early church was their commitment to connectedness—because they knew connectedness doesn't just happen. They met together every day. They ate together with glad and sincere hearts. Over time that value began to fade. So the writer of Hebrews said, "Let us consider how we may spur one another on toward love and good deeds, not giving up meeting together, as some are in the habit of doing." In other words, keep committed to community.

I've never known anyone who failed at love yet succeeded at life. I've never known anyone who succeeded at love yet failed at life. We need love to live.

Author Robert Putnam made a staggering comment in his book *Bowling Alone*: "As a rough rule of thumb, if you belong to no groups but decide to join one, you cut your risk of dying over the next year *in half*." It's difficult to imagine anyone not being interested in cutting his or her risk of dying in half. That's why the new motto for small groups at the church where I serve is, *Join a group or die*.

In sports the more encouragement that athletes need from fans, the less likely they are to get it. When a slumping player of a losing softball team comes up to bat, rarely do fans think: *Let us consider how we can spur her on to good deeds*. Too often people who need cheers the most receive them the least.

Every day, everybody you know faces life with eternity on the line, and life has a way of beating people down. Every life needs a cheering section. Every life needs a shoulder to lean on once in a while. Every life needs prayer. Every life needs a hug sometimes. Every life needs to hear a voice saying, "Don't give up."

» The Gift of Love

The deepest words of the soul are the simplest: "I love you."

I know some people grow up in homes where those words aren't heard a lot. I have three kids of my own, and I love to tell them I love them. And not just when they're doing something that makes me proud, but also when they mess up. When they're discouraged. When they feel lonely. "I'm with you. I care about you. You're not alone."

Let no debt remain outstanding, except the continuing debt to love one another, for whoever loves others has fulfilled the law. (Romans 13:8)

My mom always said two things when she was really worried. One was, "I thought you were dead in a ditch somewhere." (You'd think "dead" would be bad enough, but it's not just dead—it's "dead in a ditch." You could've been dead in a lovely meadow or something. That wouldn't be so bad, I guess. But dead in a ditch? That's awful!)

The other statement was, "I was afraid someone hit you over the head." (Not just "hit you"—that would be pretty bad. But "hit you over the head" because the head is such a vulnerable place.)

And if she were *really* worried about us, she'd combine them: "I was afraid someone hit you over the head, and you were lying dead in a ditch." These were just her ways of saying, "I love you. I'm with you."

Maybe there's someone in your life who needs you to look him or her in the eye and say: "I'm with you." The Spirit of God is at work in us all the time, prompting love all the time. And every moment is an opportunity to practice a gesture of love.

» The Gift of Belonging

When I'm loved, I belong to someone, and that person belongs to me. This is why the most common designation for a person in Jesus' community is "brother" or "sister."

That's why home and family play such important roles in our lives—even when the people in that home and family can really irritate us sometimes. And it's also why it hurts so much when a home gets messed with—either through divorce, or fighting, or stress, or pain.

The idea of a family is God's gift to us.

One day God said to the angels, "I have an idea. I'm going to create the family."

An angel asked, "What is it?"

"I'm very excited about this idea," God said. "Of course, I'm excited about all my ideas. One of the great things about being God is that you just never have a bad idea—but this one is special. *Family* is going to be the way I connect people in love. It'll work like this: Adult people will sign up to take care of tiny little strangers."

"Are they going to get paid?" the angel asked.

"No, that little stranger is actually going to cost them a lot of money. Not only that, but the little stranger won't even be able to talk at first. It will just cry and scream, and the adult people will have to guess why. It will make them lose sleep. It will make messes all the time that they have to clean up. It will be utterly helpless. In fact, they have to watch that little stranger 24 hours a day, seven days a week. Then when it's two years old, that little stranger will be able to say words like *no* and *mine*, and it will throw tantrums.

"And then I'm thinking about inventing puberty. I'm not too sure about that one yet. But if I do, the now-bigger strangers will get these things called 'hormones' that will go crazy. Odd things will happen to their bodies. They'll get pimples, their voices will crack, and they'll start to get shivers when they think about the opposite sex.

"Then they'll grow all the way up, and just when they're mature and beautiful and interesting and able to contribute—they'll move away. That's the idea. What do you all think?"

The angels shuffled around and looked at their feet. *Who's going to tell him?* they thought. Finally, one angel asked, "Lord, who would sign up for that? Why would they do it?"

Here's where God really got excited. "They won't even know why. They'll just look at that little body, those little hands and feet, and they'll think this tiny little stranger is beautiful, even though he looks like every other baby—kind of squishy and red-faced. Then one day that little stranger will smile at them, and they'll think they've won the lottery. That little stranger will say 'Dada' and 'Mama.' And then those little arms and hands will open up and reach out and wrap around the adult's neck, and that grown-up will understand for the first time why arms and hands were created.

"What it's really all about is grace.

"The little strangers will learn that they're prized and belong before they've ever done a single thing to earn it. The older generation will learn that when they give, they ultimately receive. When they give the most, they receive the most.

"And then one day I'll tell them, *Human race, I am your Father. You are my daughter; you are my son.*

"That's when they'll really Get It."

connectedness inventory

When something goes wrong, do I have at least one friend I can easily and honestly talk to about it?

Yes No

Is there a friend's home I can go to if I need a break from my own home?

Yes No

Is there someone who really knows my biggest fears and temptations?

Yes No

Do I know the biggest fears and temptations of one or more of my friends?

Yes No

Do I have a friend I trust to keep private the things I share?

Yes No

If I receive good news — like making the team or getting a good grade — do I have a friend I could call right away because I want to share my news?

Yes No

If I can't say yes to most of these questions, I may want to look for a small group to join or invite someone over as a first step to getting connected.

Chapter 16
Be Human

In the church we have a sin problem.

The problem isn't just that we sin—everyone has *that* problem.

Our problem is that we can't talk about it.

Our problem is that we pretend we *don't* have a problem. We're comfortable with stories about people who *used* to sin, and people often get invited to give their testimonies as long as they have happy endings: *I used to have a problem; but then I met God, and now I'm doing much better.*

Imagine telling a counselor, "I want to talk only about the problems I *used* to have. Please don't ask me to admit having any problems *now.* It'd be embarrassing. I'm afraid you might reject me."

Would anyone go to a counselor to try to convince the counselor that counseling isn't necessary? The answer is, of course, no.

But would anyone go to a church to try to convince the congregation that what the church can provide isn't needed? The answer is, unfortunately, yes. Many do.

People are okay telling doctors that their bodies have problems or telling mechanics that their cars have problems. Can't sinners be okay telling other sinners that they have a sin problem? If I want God (or anyone else, for that matter) to love the *real* me, then I'll have to work at getting real.

David was Israel's greatest king — but he was also a polygamist (which means he had more than one wife). He was a terrible father. He wanted another man's wife, committed adultery with her, lied to her husband, eventually had the husband murdered, and covered up his crime for a year. As a friend of mine said, no one at the time was wearing a "What Would David Do?" bracelet.

But somehow David was called "a man after [God's] own heart."

Is it possible for someone to struggle so deeply with sin yet still long for God at the same time?

I once heard a Christian leader speak about the two "great sins" in his spiritual life. He didn't boldly tell enough people about Jesus when he rode on airplanes, and his mind sometimes wandered when he prayed. He expressed great frustration over these sins.

What hope does that leave for the rest of us?

Even in writing this, I'm thinking about a strange problem. If a pastor confesses to serious sin, people usually say that pastor should leave the pastorate. If the pastor confesses only to safe, non-scandalous sins, however, people may believe the pastor is inauthentic and hypocritical. So right now I find myself wanting to make some confession that will look vulnerable and honest — but won't be so scandalous that it costs me my job. I can't confess sin without sinning in the act of confessing!

Relationships grow deep when people get real, which is to say they get honest about the sin known to us all.

» The Spirit Flows in Transparency, So Come as You Are

I have a recurring problem that sometimes requires treatment. It's a little embarrassing to mention. But recently it became very troublesome, and I had to go to the urgent care center. Andrew, the medical student on call, asked me what the problem was, and I didn't want to tell him. Want to know?

You probably don't, but I'll tell you anyhow.

I had wax in my ears that had been building up over time, and then, when I went swimming, water got behind the wax until I could barely hear. People would come up to me after church, and I couldn't tell if they were saying "hi" or confessing deep sin.

So I finally went to the urgent care center, but I didn't want to name my problem. When I at last told Andrew, my helplessness melted when he grinned.

"That's *tremendous*!" he said. "We're going to get that wax right out. I love getting wax out. It's one of the things I do best. All kinds of people have that problem. I'm a wax specialist."

Andrew took out a high-pressure hose and an ice pick and removed a piece of wax the size of a small grapefruit. He said, "Man, your body really produces a lot of wax." I felt much better, and he was so happy to get it out.

My wife used to be a nurse. So when I arrived home, she asked, "Did you bring the piece of wax home? Can I see it?"

"I just left it there," I said. "But I could go back and see if they saved it or something."

Why was I embarrassed about my wax? Andrew is my friend. My wife was so proud of me, she wanted to see it. Their acceptance helps me to accept the fact that I am a wax machine. Now I don't care who knows.

When you can step into openness and stop pretending, you find yourself coming alive. Hiding and dishonesty are always the enemies of Really Living.

There's an old story about the source of the word *sincere*. The ancient Romans used to admire the beauty of Greek marble sculptures. But the statues were already a few centuries old, and some of them had cracks or gaps in the marble. Then sellers discovered that if they put wax in the cracks and gaps, these figures looked great—for a season. The wax looked like real marble; but over time, the wax would yellow and harden until it became apparent that the statue wasn't totally authentic. So if sellers wanted to put a statue on the market, and it was all marble—the real deal through and through—they'd mark it *sine*, the Latin word for "without," and then *cera*, the Latin word for "wax."

Sine cera. Without wax. (See where this is headed?)

When the Christian church started, people met together in their homes "with glad and sincere hearts"—without wax—because now there was a circle of connectedness where everyone could come on in just as they were.

Sincere hearts are the ones with the most joy.

In writing to this early community of believers, the apostle Paul commanded, "Accept one another, then, just as Christ accepted you, in order to bring praise to God." Acceptance is more than just being liked by someone. Jesus didn't say to me, "If you just clean up a little, if you just dress better and read the Bible more, *then* I'll let you into my family." Of course he's going to help me become my best self, but I don't have to pretend to be any better than I am to be in Jesus' circle.

How did Jesus accept you? Just the way you are. When someone knows the embarrassing, crushing truth about me and still accepts me, I come alive.

» Give the Gift of Confession

One of the most important times of my spiritual life was when I sat down with a longtime friend and said, "I don't want to have any secrets anymore." I told him everything I was most ashamed of. I told him what made me jealous, what made me feel cowardly, how I hurt my wife with my anger. I told him about lies I'd told and regrets that keep me up at night. I felt vulnerable because I was afraid I was now going to be outside the circle, that I'd lose connection with him. Much to my surprise, he didn't even look away.

And I'll never forget his next words.

"I've never loved you more than I love you right now."

The exact truth about me that I thought would drive him away became a bond that drew us closer together. He then told me about secrets he'd been carrying.

I can only be loved to the level where I'm known.

If I keep part of my life a secret from you, you may tell me that you love me. But inside I really believe that you wouldn't love me if you knew the whole truth about me. I can only get love from you to the extent that I'm known by you.

I cannot be really loved unless I'm really known.

To be really known and really loved is the most healing gift one human being can give to another. James writes, "Confess your sins to one another, and pray for one another so that you may be healed." We're all forgiven, recovering sinners, and we can't be secure in a relationship if we're loved only because we're smart, pretty, strong, or successful. Sin isolates us, and sin and isolation will make us sick in our souls—even in our bodies. Confession and then prayer, connectedness to each other and to God, brings in the Spirit and helps bring healing.

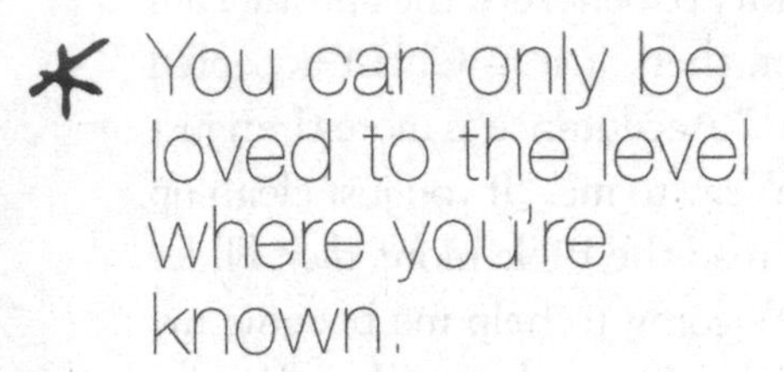

» Recognize the J-Curve

I don't know what level of math you've studied or even if you like math at all. But hang with me anyway. Experts in the learning field sometimes talk about the J-curve, a graph that measures performance where people initially do worse before they start improving. Their progress looks like a letter "J" when you graph it out, with a dip in the beginning before things head upward.

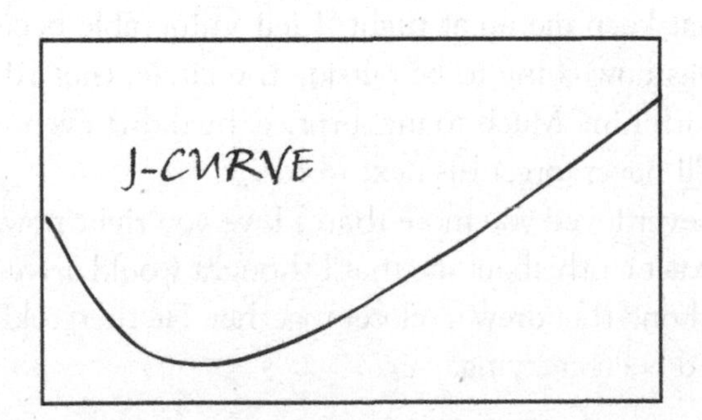

Imagine you've been hitting tennis balls the wrong way. If someone teaches you the correct grip, proper form, and right footwork, then when you start trying to hit tennis balls the right way—you'll actually hit them worse than when you were doing it the wrong way! But if you stick with it, eventually you'll play tennis far better than you used to. But you have to accept the fact that, at first, it'll be worse.

Do you remember when Jesus was walking on the water, and he called to the disciples in the boat and asked Peter to get out of the boat and walk on the water toward him? When Peter dug up enough faith to get out of the boat, he sank and looked worse than any of the other disciples. Another time Peter tried to defend Jesus by cutting off a soldier's ear with a sword. And another time Peter promised to be loyal to Jesus, but he fell flat on his faith.

Eventually, though, Peter's faith and boldness and loyalty and wisdom made it possible for him to become a leader of the church. He got worse before he got better. Yet, notice that his failings didn't shock or discourage Jesus. In fact, Jesus was so patient with his disciples that we could think of the J-curve as the "Jesus-curve." He'll never stop helping a follower who's honestly seeking to grow.

Jesus will always lead us toward growth, and growth always requires risk, and risk always means potential failure. So Jesus is always leading us into potential failure. But he never gives up on his students just because they fail.

If you haven't been confronting people when you should, and then you start to do it, you'll do it badly at first. If you've rarely encouraged people, your first tries at it might be clumsy. If you've never shared your faith, then the first time you do it you might stumble all over yourself.

Go ahead and stumble. Failure isn't falling down; real failure is when you don't even try. We ought to celebrate failure.

We're living on the J-curve.

» The Gift of Honest Language

Being human means being honest about what we want, but all too often we gloss over human difficulties with religious-sounding language. There's the story about a boy who comes home and doesn't notice that his mom is visiting with their pastor. The boy holds a dead rat in his hand. "Mom, you'll never guess what! There was a rat running around behind the garage. I saw it, and I threw a stone and hit it. It just laid there, so I went over and stomped on it. Then I picked it up and threw it against the wall as hard as I could. And I picked it up and threw it again!" Now he sees the pastor sitting there. And if looks could kill, the boy's mom would have ended his life with her stare. So the kid holds the dead rat high in the air and adds in his best religious-sounding voice, "And then the dear Lord called him home!"

When we try to look more spiritual, we actually make ourselves less human. Pretending always cuts us off from the flow of the Spirit.

If ever there were a true "just as I am" church, if ever there were a community where everybody could bring all their junk and brokenness with them without neat and tidy happy endings, if ever there was a group where everyone was loved and no one pretended—there wouldn't be a building big enough for everyone who'd want to come.

in the flow ≈

- ≈ Who is the friend I'm most honest with?
- ≈ What are my secret regrets and temptations? Is there someone I can talk with about them?
- ≈ Spend some time thinking about your regrets and temptations. Take some unhurried time to talk with the person you trust most deeply. Share — at a level that matches how well you know and trust that person — how your heart and soul are really doing.
- ≈ Laugh at yourself at least once today.

Chapter 17

Find a Few Difficult People to Help You Grow

Some people lure me out of the flow of the Spirit. They judge me, and I feel discouraged. They dislike me, and I feel rejected. They are a black hole of need, and they drain me. They throw roadblocks in front of me and discourage me. They anger me. They scare me. They depress me. (Plus, I don't like them. Big surprise, huh?)

The playwright George Bernard Shaw sat next to a snobby, boring guy at a dinner party one evening. After listening to this guy talk endlessly about useless information, Shaw said to him, "Between the two of us, we know all there is to know."

"How's that?" asked his fascinated companion.

"Well," replied Shaw, "You seem to know everything except that you're a bore. And I know that!"

We all have difficult people in our lives, but hear this: God can use them to help you become the best version of you — maybe even more effectively than the people you enjoy being around. Jesus said,

> "You're familiar with the old written law, 'Love your friend,' and its unwritten companion, 'Hate your enemy.' I'm challenging that. I'm telling you to love your enemies. Let them bring out the best in you. . . . If all you do is love the lovable, do you expect a bonus? Anybody can do that. If you simply say hello to those who greet you, do you expect a medal? Any run-of-the-mill sinner does that. In a word, what I'm saying is, Grow up. You're kingdom subjects. Now live like it. Live out your God-created identity."

Other people don't create your spirit; they uncover your spirit.

In fact, if God wants to grow some specific quality in you, God may send a person who tempts you to behave in just the opposite way. If you need to develop love, then some unlovable people may be your greatest challenge. If you need to develop hope, then keeping hope while you're around discouragers will make it strong. If you want to grow in your ability to speak up, a hard-to-confront intimidator will give you serious practice. Just like lifting weights strengthens muscles and cardio exercises strengthen hearts, difficult people can strengthen our ability to love.

Q: Why does God allow difficult people in my life?

A: Well, what other kind are there?

That's not a sarcastic answer. Think about it: If God were to get rid of all the difficult people in the world—if God were to remove everybody with faults, flaws, ugliness, and sin—you'd get awfully lonely.

We always wish that God would give us lives without difficult people. But how many great characters in the Bible had difficult people in their lives? Moses had Pharaoh, Elijah had Jezebel, Esther had Haman, Jacob had Laban, David had Saul, John the Baptist had Herod. Even Jesus had Judas. If God loves you and wants to shape you, God will send some difficult people your way. But take heart: *You're the difficult person God is sending to shape somebody else!*

If we can learn to have rivers of living water flowing through us in these relationships, we'll be unstoppable.

» Recognize the Impact

We're far more affected by the people in our lives than most of us realize. We're always—*always!*—being energized or drained by every interaction.

Dr. Jill Bolte Taylor was a 37-year-old, Harvard-trained brain scientist when she suffered a massive stroke. The left side of her brain, which controls speech and linear thinking, was devastated. For many months she lay in a hospital bed, unable to have a conversation with anyone. She writes about how even though she couldn't understand the words people were saying to her, she became extremely aware of whether the people approaching her were increasing her sense of life or lessening it.

> I experienced people as concentrated packages of energy. . . . Although I could not understand the words they spoke, I could read volumes from their facial expression and body language. I paid very close attention to how energy dynamics affected me. I realized that some people brought me energy while others took it away.

At a level deeper than words, deeper than exchanging information, each interaction with another person is a spiritual exchange. Some people are life-bringers: They increase our energy, deepen our hope, add to our joy, and call out the best in us. Other people are life-drainers: They add to our anxiety and invite us toward cynicism. We find ourselves becoming defensive, depressed, or frustrated when they're around.

How do we grow through difficult relationships?

» Keeping God between You and Me

Before some friends of mine went on a trip, they dropped off their hunting dog at a summer camp for dogs. I didn't even know there were such places. It was a refresher course on obedience school to retrain their dog and make sure that every time he gets a command, his response is quick, enthusiastic, unquestioning obedience. When the dog came home, it was as if he were a new creature. It was summer camp and reform school all wrapped into one.

Wouldn't it be nice if there were such places for people? If there were, they'd be full. Of course, that's what really kills us — we can't fix *people*. There's a good reason for this, though: Everyone has a soul. Everyone has a place deep inside where only that person and God can meet. We may think, *I can intimidate, lecture, sweet-talk, manipulate, persuade, reward, or withdraw to get the behavior I want out of that person*. And maybe I can, but only on the outer edges of that individual's personality. I can't touch the deepest part of another person. Only God can do that.

Prayer is the closest we come to influencing people at their deepest levels — to go with God into another person's soul — because Jesus always stands between me and the innermost parts of another person. The most direct way to affect another person isn't talking to that person; the most direct way is talking to Jesus.

I can remember so clearly the hardest conversation I've ever had. It was with a person I'd known for more than a decade, and we were talking about some complicated, longtime problems in our relationship. I'd avoided speaking truthfully about our problems for years, so picking up the phone to talk felt like the hardest thing ever. I was afraid the conversation would be exhausting and painful, that we wouldn't see eye to eye.

It ended up being worse than that!

But here was the one thought that made it possible for me to have the talk: *I don't have to control the outcome. I don't have to make the other person agree. I just have to show up. The rest is up to God.*

At the end of the conversation, even though it didn't end the way I wished, I felt alive because I was trusting Jesus with a challenging relationship.

» What Makes Someone Difficult for You?

A whole lot of studies have been done on what causes us to like other people. Out of all the possible causes — physical attractiveness,

IQ, ability, personality type—the number-one factor that determines if we like another person is the degree to which that person likes us. If someone likes you, then you'll probably like that person. If someone doesn't like you, then you probably won't like that person, either.

This is humbling.

If someone I've never liked says something good about me, I think, *Man! This person is cooler than I thought.*

God's not that way, though. God loves people who love him, of course; but God also loves people who don't love him. God doesn't love them because he has to. God doesn't say to himself, *Well, I'm God, so I guess I'm stuck having to love people. Boy, I sure wish I didn't have to!*

God does it because love is the only way to life.

» Staying in the Flow of the Spirit Takes a Quarter-Second

Anger can take me out of the Spirit's flow. This is why Paul writes, "Do not grieve the Holy Spirit of God [in other words, don't cut yourself off from the flow of the Spirit], with whom you were sealed for the day of redemption. Get rid of all bitterness, rage and anger, brawling and slander, along with every form of malice."

Difficult relationships can give the Evil One a grip on us, but God has wired us so that in times of intense difficulty, we have a kind of built-in moment to turn to the Spirit for help.

Let's say I decide that I'm going to move my hand, and that impulse travels from my brain to the hand through my nerves. But in between the brain activity and the movement of the hand is what one researcher calls the "life-giving quarter-second."

There is a quarter-second between when that impulse takes place in your brain and when that action takes place in your body. And that quarter-second—although it doesn't sound like very long in the life of the mind—is huge.

The apostle Paul wrote, "'In your anger do not sin' ..." and do not give the devil a foothold." That one quarter of a second is the time when the Holy Spirit can take control. That's when you can give the grip to the Holy Spirit, or you can give it to sin. That one quarter-second in your mind can be an opportunity to say, "Spirit, I've got this impulse right now; should I act on it?"

Imagine that my little brother or my parent or my friend angers me, and some heated words form in the back of my head. There's a life-giving quarter-second, but I blow right past it. I'm frustrated. And I use language that I never thought I'd use.

It's amazing how the desire to hurt someone you love can be felt so strongly in your body one moment and then lead to such pain when you let it fly. But the good news is that when you blow it—and you *will* blow it—God sends another quarter-second right behind the first one.

And you can get right back into the flow.

» Learning from the Master

No one mastered the art of dealing with difficult people better than Jesus did. He had lots of practice. The Romans wanted to silence him; Herod wanted to kill him; religious leaders envied him; his family thought he'd lost his mind; the townspeople wanted to stone him; Judas betrayed him; soldiers beat him; the crowds shouted for his crucifixion; and his own disciples ran out on him. But Jesus never prayed for God to remove difficult people from his life.

If he had, there would have been no people left at all.

Jesus' teachings about dealing with difficult people flowed out of deep and painful experience and wisdom. Let's look at his teaching about how you deal with people who'd try to use you.

Users

Jesus gives this example: "If anyone forces you to go one mile, go with them two miles." His listeners would've understood this situation well. In those days if Roman soldiers were carrying any kind of a load, they were allowed to randomly force the Jews to carry that load for them for a mile.

This is the kind of person who'd use us, thinking of us not as people but as tools. What do you do in that situation? Jesus invites people to see their enemies as human beings. This Roman soldier is a young boy, a stranger, probably poor himself. All he gets from the locals is unfriendliness. So here's an idea: You finish the mile, look him in the eye, and say, "You look tired. Can I give you a little more help? Can I go with you another mile?"

That response would blow the soldier's mind. Nobody does that! It's like paying for a speeding ticket and sending a tip along with it.

Oftentimes when someone is being difficult, I want to think of that person as purposely unlikable rather than as a real person with his or her own story. A friend offered to introduce English essayist Charles Lamb to a guy whom Lamb had disliked for a long time—not because Lamb knew him, but only because of what Lamb had heard about him. "Don't make me meet him," Lamb said. "I want to go on hating him, and I can't do that to a man I know."

We can give the gift of understanding. We remember that the people we don't like are also human beings. We put ourselves in their place. We take the time to imagine how they feel, how they're treated. We ask what would help them become the best versions of themselves, and, in turn, the interaction becomes an opportunity for me to practice becoming the best version of myself. We actually *need* difficult people to reach our full potential.

» Being the "Difficult Person"

I once gave a talk about difficult people that I thought was terrific. That is, until I found out that someone I knew quite well and worked with closely had told a mutual friend who his difficult person was. Me.

He wasn't a casual acquaintance, either. That means I'd been speaking and acting in ways that were painful and life-draining to someone quite close to me. Our conversations often left him feeling as though he was just an audience. I was sending clear signals that I thought my opinions were more accurate and important than his. All of this left him wanting to hide. On top of that, I'd been clueless.

My own defensiveness and embarrassment made me want to hide, too. We were able to overcome this somewhat, but I've never forgotten the emotion of discovering that I was someone else's difficult person. I hope it's made me more aware in other relationships. I know it's made me more grateful for grace.

When given the choice, I'd always rather hang out with my favorite people in the world than the ones I find difficult. It'd be kind of weird if I didn't! But just remember: God can use those thorny relationships to help you become the best version of you.

PART SIX

transforming my experience

Chapter 18

You've Gotta Go through Some Junk before You Come Back Home

Here's a crazy thought: Imagine that when you were born, someone handed a script of your entire life to your parents. The whole story of everything you'd experience, written out just like a story. But then, even better, the same person who handed them the script also gave them an eraser and five minutes to delete whatever future "happenings" they wanted to remove.

Your parents might read about a really difficult situation that you'd go through in elementary school. They might read about some skill that comes easily for some kids, but it's going to be more difficult for you. They could read about you making a great circle of friends in high school—only to have one of them die of cancer. After high school, they read that you get into the college you wanted to attend, but you're hurt in a car accident while you're there. Following college, they read that you go through a tough time of depression. Then they read that a few years later, you get a great job—but soon lose that job because the economy hits a rough spot. They read that you get married but go through the grief of separation a few years later.

If your parents had this script of your life in front of them and five minutes to delete hard things so you wouldn't have to go through them, *what hard things should they erase?* That's the question psychologist Jonathan Haidt asked in this hypothetical exercise. *Wouldn't you want them to take out all the stuff that causes you pain?*

We live in a generation of "helicopter parents" ready to swoop into their children's lives to make sure no one is mistreating them and no one gets in their way of experiencing success after success in school, sports, and relationships. Whoa! If your parents could've waved a wand and erased every failure, disappointment, and misery, are you sure it would be a good idea? Would such deletions allow you to grow into the best version of yourself? Is it possible that in some ways people actually *need* hard times and setbacks—maybe even suffering—to reach the fullest level of growth?

The apostle Paul believed that as we live in the flow of the Spirit, suffering can lead to growth. Suffering can actually produce more people who Really Live.

> We rejoice in the hope of the glory of God. Not only so, but we also rejoice in our sufferings, because we know that suffering produces perseverance; perseverance, character; and character, hope. And hope does not disappoint us, because God has poured out his love into our hearts by the Holy Spirit, whom he has given us. (Romans 5:2–5 NIV)

» Three Attitudes toward Hard Times

There are a lot of ways to look at the ups and downs of our futures, and philosopher Robert Roberts describes three attitudes we can hold: Hope, despair, and resignation.

Hope is the belief that my future holds good possibilities. I really *desire* what I think this future holds, and I *believe* this future possibility to be on the way. Hope is not hype. Of course, hope involves waiting, and hope can include uncertainty, so it can be scary. But when I hope, I get excited just thinking about the future. I welcome tomorrow. You can always tell if you're around a hopeful human.

Despair, on the other hand, creeps in if I really want something but believe deep down that it won't happen. In despair, my wishing is still strong, but I believe my wishes will be unfulfilled. The thought of the future becomes painful: *This depression will never go away. I'll never be loved.* Despair paralyzes. The soul can't survive for very long with deep despair. Despair is so poisonous that people will manage it by *resignation*.

Resignation is a kind of middle ground between *hope* and *despair*. In resignation, I shrink down my desire, trying to convince myself that what I really wanted so much isn't a big deal. *The team isn't that great. She's not that pretty, and there are plenty of other girls around.* When it comes to dealing with situations that seem sure to disappoint (like being a Chicago Cubs baseball fan), learning to accept the inevitable with calmness seems like the wisest thing to do. But can resignation alone keep your life going?

The best version of you is a hoper because the Spirit of life is a Spirit of hope. The Spirit never leads us to despair, and there is always hope—which isn't based on specific situations, but instead is an inner quality. In fact, researchers have identified something in people's personalities that they call *dispositional optimism*—the ability to be hopeful of the future.

Give yourself a five-second hope test by answering yes or no to these two statements:

- In uncertain times, I usually expect the best.
- If something can go wrong for me, it usually will.

If you answered yes to the first question and no to the second, you'll naturally love this chapter. If you answered any other way, then you *need* this chapter because the good news about hope is that it can be learned!

» Normal Life and Crisis

In what we call "normal life," we drift along assuming certain things that might end up working for quite a while: I may feel secure because my family has a certain amount of money. I have an identity because I get good grades, or I'm on a certain team, or I date a certain person. I have a purpose because I'm going to achieve more than I already have. Life seems to "work."

Then a crisis comes along. Maybe your parents divorce. Maybe you lose someone you love. Maybe your parent loses a job. A friendship that you counted on for years suddenly ends. There is a scandal and you lose your reputation. Someone you dated for a long time looks at you and says, "It's over. It's nothing you did, but I just want to be friends. It's not you, it's me."

Any crisis carries with it this important question: *What can I build my life on that changing situations can't steal from me? What really matters?*

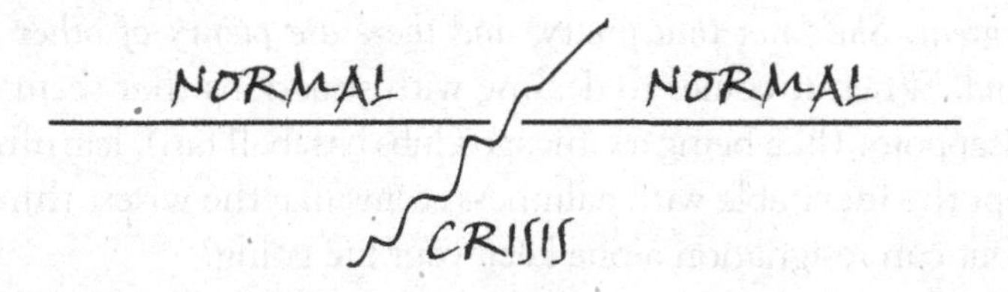

A while ago someone came into my office and told me I needed to check the rear passenger tire on my car. It looked like it was getting low, so I took it to the service station to get it patched. After a few months, somebody else told me the same thing. For several months I had to reinflate the tire, only to have it slowly leak out the new air. Eventually the car doctor said, "This tire is tired and worn out. It's time to face reality: You have to get a new tire."

Then last weekend my car wouldn't start. It was a battery problem. I thought I could get the battery recharged, but the car doctor said, "This battery is tired and worn out. It's time to face reality: You have to get a new battery."

At breakfast, after too much coffee and too little sleep the night before, I noticed my wife was looking at me in a gentle way. I asked her, "What are you thinking?"

"You're looking tired and worn out," she said.

I remembered where I'd heard those words recently, and I didn't like where this was heading.

What do you do with a broken person? I can admit to myself that sometimes a tire can't be reinflated or a battery can't be recharged. But what if the problem is closer to home? Ernest Hemingway wrote, "Sooner or later, the world breaks everyone, and those who are broken are strongest in the broken places." (Think about that one.)

Sometimes that's true. But sometimes people write beautiful things and believe they're true—or hope they're true—but they don't help. Hemingway himself had a brokenness that couldn't get stronger, and he ended up killing himself because the pain seemed too great.

Something happens to us in the middle of hard times.

For a long time researchers studied what enables some people to tolerate suffering. But over the last decade or so, the focus has shifted from looking only at how some people make it through to how people can endure hard times and actually come out on the other side stronger than before.

One line of thinking is that hard times *can* lead to growth. Another line of thinking is that the highest levels of growth can't be achieved *without* hard times. It may be that somehow hard times lead to growth in ways that no other circumstances produce.

But hard times don't automatically bring growth. They can cripple people, and much of the outcome depends on how people respond to adversity. Jonathan Haidt writes about three ways that this growth can happen. I adjust them here a bit, add a fourth, and look at how God can grow us in hard times.

1. Rising to a challenge uncovers abilities hidden within you (and beyond you!) that would otherwise have stayed hidden.

It's in hard times that we find out what we're really made of, just like we find out what's inside a tube of toothpaste when it gets squeezed. A lot of times people say, "I could never go through what that person went through. I'd die." But then they go through it and—lo and behold!—their hearts keep beating. Their world goes on.

We don't know what we're capable of until we have to deal with what we've never dealt with before.

I can't guarantee that my situation will work out the way I want it to, but I can always ask, "How would the person I most want to emulate face this situation?"

Nowhere do we see this idea highlighted more significantly than in the Bible. God could've let Abraham stay in the comfort of Ur, Moses stay in the splendor of Pharaoh's courts, and Aaron stay in the safety of the crowd. He could have kept David away from Goliath; Shadrach, Meshach, and Abednego out of the fiery furnace; Daniel out of the lion's den; Elijah away from Jezebel; Nehemiah out of detention; Jonah out of the whale; John the Baptist away from Herod; Esther from being threatened; Jeremiah from being rejected; and Paul from being shipwrecked. But God didn't. In fact, God used each of these hardships to bring each of these people closer to him—and to create perseverance, character, and hope in them.

A classic Bible story about dealing with hard times involves Joseph (the Old Testament Joseph in Genesis). At the beginning of his life, Joseph dreamed about being the one everybody bows down to—helped a lot by the fact that he was the favorite son of his father, which made his brothers envy him. Then Joseph was kidnapped by his own brothers and ended up working as a slave in Potiphar's house. Joseph lost his home, his security, and his status as favorite son. What does Joseph have left? He was in a strange bed, in a strange house, in a strange land, with no friends, no clue about his future, and no explanation. But Joseph had one gift—and that one thing made all the difference.

Scripture says, "The LORD was with Joseph."

Joseph was not alone.

What happens to someone who loses everything but God, then finds out that God is actually enough? As a powerless stranger, Joseph feels the presence of God in a way he never did while in the comfort of his own home. Rivers of living water that he'd never known before began flowing from his belly because hope comes from the promise that "we know that in all things God works for the good of those who love him." God wasn't at work creating the situations Joseph wanted—but God was at work in bad situations creating the *Joseph* that God wanted.

> God isn't at work creating the situations you want—but God is at work in bad situations creating the *you* that God wants.

Sometimes people quote a "verse" from the Bible—except it's not even a real verse! One of the most misquoted "verses" you'll never find in the Bible is: "God will never give me more than I can handle."

Huh?

Are you kidding me? Where's that one? Poverty, holocausts, racism, war—people are given more than they can handle all the time!

The Bible *does* say, however, that no temptation is given to people without a way out—but that verse is about temptation, not hard times. The Bible does *not* promise that you'll only be given what you can handle. In fact, the one certainty of everybody's life is that you'll die—and you definitely can't handle that! Instead you'll never be placed in a situation that *God* can't handle. Nothing—including death—will place you beyond God's flow of living waters.

Maybe you're in a situation right now—involving friends, family, finances—that's not what you wanted. Maybe you want to lie down and give up. But when you don't give up—when you show up, when you offer the best you have—something good happens *inside* of you that far outweighs whatever's happening *outside* of you.

Jesus faced adversity when he told his followers that if they had faith, they could command a mountain and it would be cast into the sea. When my focus is on the mountain, I'm driven by my fear. When my focus is on God, though, I'm made alive by my faith. But if I didn't have the mountain, I'd never know that faith could be in me.

Your situations—even the best of them—are temporary. But you—the person you become—will go on forever.

2. Adversity can deepen relationships.

Somehow suffering can soften a heart and deepen friendships in a unique way.

Nancy went to nursing school with a classmate I'll call Shelly. She was intelligent, engaging, and beautiful—everyone loved her.

Shelly fell in love with and married a guy I'll call Steve. He was an architect and a basketball player who looked like he should be on the cover of a magazine. They had more good genes than any couple has a right to expect. But when Shelly walked into her bridal shower, she was sad that everything wasn't as it should be: She'd broken a fingernail while pumping gas.

"But it's okay," she said in her deep Southern drawl. "Steve said that once we're married, I'll never have to put gas in my car again."

Does that make anyone else want to puke?

On that day a tough situation was a broken nail. But storms have a way of coming into every life.

After they were married Shelly and Steve wanted to have kids. But they were disappointed when they couldn't get pregnant for years. They felt the pain of watching other people walk behind baby strollers and complain about their babies not letting them get enough sleep. They wished that little cries would keep them up at night.

Finally, Shelly got pregnant, and she gave birth to a little girl.

The next month, Steve was hurt while playing basketball and knocked unconscious. In the emergency room, the doctor took one look at his X-rays and turned pale: "Don't move; don't breathe deep; don't even have a deep thought," the specialist pleaded.

The staff put him in traction and flew in a surgeon who told Steve that if he'd so much as sneezed or turned the wrong way, he could have ended up completely paralyzed or dead. Steve was at risk of dying during the operation, too.

But he didn't die—the surgery was a success.

The next month Shelly called to tell us she was pregnant again. They hadn't planned on this one. A few weeks later she called back, and for the first 30 seconds of the phone conversation, all she could do was cry.

The baby, while still inside of her, had been diagnosed with severe heart defects and massive brain issues. A lot of Steve and Shelly's friends didn't know how to appropriately respond. Some said, "Your baby will be healed. God has told us. You just have to have faith. We'll pray—you watch."

Steve and Shelly watched. They prayed. The baby wasn't healed. Everything the doctors said came true.

Others said, "People will be watching you. Don't cry. Don't look sad. Show how much faith you have."

Another person actually said, "God must love you very much to give you a retarded child." I won't even tell you what that response did to them.

If they were writing these words, Steve and Shelly would write that their little baby is precious to them beyond words. They'd write that they've grown through this pain.

They'd also write that they'd give all their growth back in a heartbeat if it meant health and wholeness for their child.

Loss isn't simply something to be recovered from. Hope doesn't mean getting back to happiness as soon as possible. God comes to us in our sadness and shares it. In that shared grief, we find love. "Mourn with those who mourn," Paul says. Love realized in the midst of shared suffering and broken souls is like no other kind of love.

One of the most common results of people who go through deep sadness is that they acquire deeper appreciation for others. People who have a serious illness often describe this crazy experience. They hate having their bodies invaded by the illness, but they wake up to how much people matter. They quit wasting time and emotion on what doesn't count.

God comes to us in our sadness and pain; and because God shares our sadness and pain, it begins to mix ever so slightly with hope.

We hang onto each other, and love surfaces in shared suffering and broken souls like no other kind of love.

As a young woman, Joni Eareckson Tada became paralyzed and has been in a wheelchair for decades. She'd tell you that she wishes every day that she could walk. She'd also tell you that she's met God and loved people in ways she couldn't have imagined apart from her wheelchair. God has used her to inspire thousands of people in ways that never would've happened except for that chair. That chair is part of the curse. And yet Joni still thanks God for the chair.

3. Adversity can change your views about what really matters.

A friend named Bill Dallas wrote a book, *Lessons from San Quentin*, about how his greatest suffering became the turning point of his life. He'd been living for money, possessions, success, beauty, pleasure, and parties—and doing really well in his quest. But Bill took a few wrong turns, made some financial decisions that weren't honest, and ended up in the San Quentin prison. But then the strangest thing happened.

He met God. Bill found a group of men who were in prison for life, and yet they'd found God. More than that, these inmates had a greater sense of peace and a deeper experience of community than the richest people he'd known on the outside. More and more, these men were becoming the best versions of themselves.

As with Joseph, the Lord was with Bill in prison. Bill says that if he were to visit one more place before he dies, it wouldn't be the Eiffel Tower or the Great Wall of China or Disney World. It would be that prison cell where he met God.

Suffering helps us to see the foolishness of chasing after temporary stuff. And when people suffer, they often make up their minds not to return to their old ways when things go back to normal. But the key is taking action before normal life takes over again. We have a short timeframe in which to make changes, or else we'll just drift back to our old patterns. Bill changed his lifestyle, his friends, his habits, his job, and his God so that when he was released from prison, his life normalized—but his values and the whole direction of his life had been transformed well beforehand.

In the end, tough times can produce hope because of a reality that's much larger than you and me.

That reality is that God is a redemptive God.

4. Adversity points us to the hope beyond ourselves.

Have you ever been to an arcade? There's something really cool about a room full of Skee-Ball tables, Pop-A-Shot basketball and Whac-a-Mole games, claw machines, and all the rest. There's magic in having your pockets full of tokens or quarters and running around like a maniac trying to get high scores and outdo your friends.

But the best kinds of arcades are the ones that give tickets! You can walk around and observe people who are already playing, while trying to decide which games offer the best chance of getting not just a ticket or two or three, but a whole string of tickets. Enough tickets that you have to wad them all up in your hand; enough that it makes it tough to dig another quarter out of your pocket for the next game.

But the point isn't to leave the arcade with a pocket jammed with tickets, right? Somewhere in the arcade is the glass countertop, and underneath that is a truckload of plastic toys—most of them worth much less than a quarter. (Unless you've saved 17 million tickets, which is the "price" listed underneath the small TV in the corner.)

So you take these tickets to the guy behind the glass counter to be exchanged. Redeemed. The redemption center is where you cash in your tickets for the prize you want.

God waited since the beginning of history—watching, suffering, loving—until in the fullness of time, he sent his only Son to a redemption center on a hill called Calvary. What does God want to redeem? *Everything.* All creation is groaning for redemption, Paul writes. God wants to redeem you.

When your situation looks depressing, when your grades are down or your confidence is sinking or your circle of friends is shrinking or your family is collapsing, you may wonder, *Is* anything *going up?*

Yes.

The chance to trust God when trusting isn't easy is wide open. The outlook for showing hope to a hope-needy world is rising higher. And the possibility of growing a storm-proof faith is always going up. This is so because certain truths remain unchanged: God is supreme, grace beats sin, prayers get heard, the Bible endures, the cross still shows the power of sacrificial love, the tomb is still empty, and the kingdom that Jesus announced is still expanding without needing to be bailed out by human efforts.

God is still in the business of redemption, specializing in bringing something very, very good out of something very, very bad.

PART SEVEN

flowing from here on out

Chapter 19

Ask for a Mountain

Big corporations spend millions of dollars to find just the right icon that communicates — in memorable and compelling ways — what the companies offer.

For instance, Nike's logo is a little checkmark-looking symbol called a "swoosh." It's actually a stylized version of the wing from the Greek statue *Winged Victory*. The word *nike* itself is from the Greek word for "victory." Nike's logo is a swoosh; their brand is *success*.

Apple's logo is, well, an apple. An Internet story says it came from the Bible's tree of knowledge, but that may be an urban myth. Yet the logo has come to represent the meeting of technology and intelligence like no other symbol, ever. Apple's icon is an apple; their brand is *smart*.

McDonald's logo is one of the best known and most recognized in the world — the Golden Arches. On every continent the arches convey joy and fulfillment — the Happy Meal. McDonald's logo is a giant yellow "M"; their brand is *pleasure*.

If you were to choose a logo for your life, what would it be?

All three of the aforementioned logos are known around the planet, but none is the *most* famous logo in the world. There's one symbol that's been around for centuries. You see it on tombstones and T-shirts and chapels and necklaces—and in countless other settings.

The cross.

Because it's been around so long, people look at the cross without thinking about what it means. Many think of it as just a piece of jewelry. There's a story about a woman who walks into a jewelry store and asks for a cross. The clerk replies, "Do you want an empty one, or one with a little man on it?"

The cross was not empty.

The cross represents a cruel method of execution—crucifixion. It was invented by the Persians and popularized by Alexander the Great, but perfected by the Romans as a means of preventing rebellion. It was designed to be both painful and humiliating; the English word *excruciating* comes from the Latin word for "crucifixion."

Jesus said, "Whoever wants to be my disciple must deny themselves and take up their cross and follow me." This was the image that came to represent the movement associated with Jesus.

Think about how strange this is: A minuscule movement called "Christianity" is struggling under huge adversity and trying to attract converts, yet the symbol they chose to represent their message wasn't an icon conveying success, knowledge, pleasure, or power. They chose a symbol universally understood to represent shame, failure, and death.

Who'd choose a means of execution as their company logo? Imagine the electric company hiring an advertising consultant who advises them to make their primary image a tiny electric chair—complete with a catchy little slogan underneath: THE POWER IS ON.

When Jesus invited his followers to "take up their cross," it wasn't an invitation to destruction. It was a call to spiritual greatness through this amazing thing called sacrificial love. Human beings were offered a cause worth living for, dying for, and being brought back to life for. God was reconciling all things to himself; evil, sin, death, and guilt were about to get kicked out.

The cross wasn't empty. There was a man on it.

Now you and I have something worth living for, dying for, and being brought back to life for—something more than success, smarts, pleasure, or power. The God of the cross is renewing and creating all things to Really Live through the power of sacrificial love.

And we get to be a part of it.

» Ask God for a Glorious Burden

We sometimes wish we had problem-free lives—except that problem-free lives would produce death by boredom. It's by working to solve problems and overcome challenges that we become the people God wants us to be. Every problem is an invitation from the Spirit. And when we say yes, we're in the flow of the Spirit.

So don't ask for comfort. Don't ask for ease. Don't ask for manageable. Ask to be given a vision for a challenge bigger than yourself—one that can make a difference in the world, one that needs the best you have to give (and then leave some space for God besides). Ask for a task that keeps you learning and growing and uncomfortable and hungry.

We can't grow apart from challenges to what's familiar and comfortable to us. The Spirit leads us into adventure. The Spirit leads us into a dangerous world. To ask for the Spirit is to ask for risk.

A family friend decided to legally change his name. Actually, he was leaving his first and last name alone but wanted to add a middle name: *Danger.* (I'm serious! This is a true story—I've seen the paperwork—*Austin Powers* comparisons notwithstanding.) He felt as though he'd always been a compliant, middle-of-the-road, play-it-safe kind of person, and he wanted to do something to stake out a new identity.

It requires a lot of legal work to get your name changed, and this friend had to go to court multiple times. On the day of his final court appearance, he was last person on the schedule. One of the cases before his involved two people who were suing each other—and they got so violent toward each other that they had to be escorted from the courtroom.

After the judge approved the name change and as my friend was walking out the door, one of the courtroom officers stopped him. "Be careful," he said. "Those two men who got kicked out have started fighting in the parking lot. It's dangerous out there."

My friend knew this was a fantastic opportunity, and he showed the officer his paperwork. "It's okay," he said. "*Danger* is my middle name."

The Spirit wants to make you a dangerous person. The Spirit wants to make you threatening to all the forces of evil and injustice and laziness that keep our world from Really Living. The Spirit wants to make you dangerously rebellious in a broken world.

It's time to ask God for a mountain.

» Finding Your Challenge

Caleb was one of 12 spies sent to explore the Promised Land after Israel left Egypt. When the spies returned, 10 of them said the mission was impossible to pull off, and they should all return to slavery in Egypt. Only Caleb and Joshua trusted God and said, "We can certainly do it."

Because of the unbelief of his people, Caleb had to spend 40 years of his life wandering through the wilderness. By the time the Israelites crossed the Jordan River, Caleb was 80 years old. Then another five years passed before the tribes of Israel were assigned plots of land in which to live. As Caleb described it years later:

> *"I was forty years old when Moses . . . sent me from Kadesh Barnea to explore the land. And I brought him back a report according to my convictions, but the others who went up with me made the hearts of the people melt in fear. I, however, followed the LORD my God wholeheartedly."*

If you have a negative attitude and a small faith when you're 40, there's a good chance you won't have a negative attitude and a small faith when you're 85 because there's a really good chance you won't ever *make it* to 85.

A psychologist named Martin Seligman studied several hundred people in a religious community and divided them into quarters from most to least optimistic and faith-filled. He found that 90 percent of the most optimistic, faith-filled people were still alive at the age of 85. But only 34 percent of the most negative, pessimistic people made it to that age.

Another study, the largest of its kind, tracked more than 2,000 adults over the age of 65 in the United States. Optimistic people—faith-filled people—had better health habits, lower blood pressure, and tougher immune systems and were half as likely to die in the next year as negative people. If you have a positive attitude, you're likely to live a decade longer than people with a negative attitude. Are you happy to hear that? If you're feeling negative about it, you could be in serious trouble.

Twelve spies went out, but only Joshua and Caleb had faith. "We can do it!" they said. "Let's go do it!" But the other 10 said, "It can't be done. Let's go back and be slaves in Egypt." Forty-five years later, Caleb was as fired up as ever. Want to guess what had happened to the other 10 scouts by then? They were all dead. None of them made it to Caleb's age.

Faith is an amazing life-giver.

Once there was a woman named Evelyn Brand. When she was young, she felt called by God to go to India. As a single woman in 1909, a calling like that required a truckload of faith and an equal amount of determination. She married a young man named Jessie, and together they began a ministry to people in rural India, bringing them education and medical supplies, and building roads to reduce the isolation of the poor.

Early in their ministry, they went seven years without having a single person understand the real message of Jesus. But then a priest of a local tribal religion developed a fever and grew deathly ill. Nobody else would go near him, but Evelyn and Jessie nursed him as he was dying. He said, "This God, Jesus, must be the true God because only Jessie and Evelyn will care for me in my dying."

The priest gave his children to them to care for after he died—and that became a spiritual turning point in that part of the world. People began to really look at the life and teachings of Jesus, and more and more started to follow him. Evelyn and Jessie had 13 years of productive service, and then Jessie died. By this time Evelyn was 50 years old, and everyone expected her to go back to her home in England. But she wouldn't do it. She was as feisty as Caleb.

She was known and loved for miles around as "Granny Brand," and she stayed another 20 years. Her son, Paul, came over when she was 70 years old, and this is what he said about his mom: "This is how to grow old. Allow everything else to fall away until those around you see only love."

» Do Something Difficult

Caleb's desire for challenge was both God's gift to him and his gift to God. As he prepared to enter the Promised Land, this is what Caleb said:

> *So here I am today, eighty-five years old! I am still as strong today as the day Moses sent me out; I'm just as vigorous to go out to battle now as I was then. Now give me this hill country that the LORD promised me that day. You yourself heard then that the Anakites were there and their cities were large and fortified, but, the LORD helping me, I will drive them out just as he said.*

Hill country is much more difficult to occupy than flat ground, but that's exactly what Caleb asked for—the hardest challenge. He had to face the Anakites, Israel's most terrifying opponents, the ones talked about in Numbers 13, of whom the people said, "We even saw descendants of Anak there. We seem like grasshoppers next to them."

Caleb asked for the hardest enemies—in the most dangerous territory.

You'd think an 85-year-old would ask for a nice condo at Hallelujah Pines Retirement Home, but he wanted the privilege of a really hard assignment. He chose another battle before he checked out. *God, just give me the hill country.*

» "Give Me the Hill Country, God"

God has wired us so that our bodies, minds, and spirits need challenges, and we especially Really Live when we face challenges for causes bigger than ourselves. We experience the flow of the Spirit most when we focus on challenges that make our communities better, and when we stop being worried about our own advancement.

When Joshua — the other faithful spy besides Caleb — became the new leader of Israel following Moses' death, Caleb could have withdrawn or moped. Instead he dug in to help the people around him.

When we take on challenges to help people around us, it actually connects us to them. If we just chase comfort, though, it leads to isolation and loneliness — and isolation is deadly.

Marian Diamond, a brilliant researcher on aging at the University of California at Berkeley, found that intentional challenges are needed to keep our brains healthy and developing. In an experiment one group of rats was given food directly, while another group had obstacles placed in front of their food dishes. The rats that had to overcome obstacles actually had their brains grow stronger, and they found their way through other mazes more quickly than the comfortable rats. The fewer problems a rat had, the faster its brain went downhill. (So if you love a rat, give it problems to solve.)

Diamond also wanted to explore the effects of isolation and loneliness in relation to aging. She found that if 12 rats were in a cage together — a little community of rats — and given challenges, their brains grew more than if they were each given a challenge in complete isolation. Then she wanted to see how this worked with older rats, so she used rats that were 600 days or older — the equivalent of a 60-year-old human. Same results.

Diamond was invited to present her research in Germany, and she found that the German rats lived to be 800 days old. This bothered Diamond because her rats started dying up to 200 days earlier. So she told her researchers that they should start giving their rats an additional item they haven't yet received — love. The rats faced the same challenges as before; but after each challenge, the researchers picked up the rats in their hands, pressed them against their lab coats, petted them, and spoke kindly to them. They'd say, "You are one sweet rat," or whatever it is you say to encourage rodents.

When the scientists started loving their lab rats, those critters did more than break the 800-day barrier. At 904 days not only were they still alive, but they were still developing stronger brains as well.

> "Listen to me, house of Jacob ... Even to your old age and gray hairs I am he, I am he who will sustain you. I have made you and I will carry you; I will sustain you and I will rescue you." (Isaiah 46:3–4)

Life isn't about comfort. It's about saying, "God, give me another mountain." It might look like Granny Brand. It might look like Caleb. It might be a story that a lot of people end up hearing about—or it might not. No one may know about your story but you and God. It doesn't matter.

Living the adventure God planned—becoming the person God created you to be—isn't just one quest among many. It's why you were born.

It's worth wanting above all else.

» Knowing Your Mountain

How will you recognize your mountain? Well, there's no formula. Just like every other area of your growth, your mountain won't look exactly like anyone else's. But often you'll recognize it because it combines the stuff that you're best at with the stuff you care most about. Yet know this for sure: *God has a mountain with your name on it.*

When Rich Stearns was a new Christian, he got engaged. His fiancée wanted to register for china, but he said to her, "As long as there are children starving in the world, we will not own china, crystal, or silver." Then, as he entered the corporate world and started climbing the ladder, he figured out that he had fantastic gifts of leadership. He loved strategic thinking, team-building, and mission achievement. Twenty years later he became the CEO of Lenox. Do you know what they manufacture? They're the top producer of luxury dishes and fine china in the country. Hmm.

One day he got a phone call from an organization called World Vision. Their mission is to fight poverty and injustice in the world, and they asked if he'd consider leaving his job and getting involved with them. So Rich went to Uganda, a country in Africa that's been devastated by the AIDS pandemic. In one of the villages there, he sat in a thatched hut with a 13-year-old boy who shared his first name—Richard. One pile of stones outside the door to the hut marked where the boy's father, who'd died of AIDS, was buried; another pile of stones marked where his mother, who'd also died of AIDS, was buried. That kind of thing happens every day in Africa.

Rich talked for a while with this young boy—who was now trying to raise his two younger brothers—and asked him at one point, "Do you have a Bible?"

"Yes," the boy said. And he went into the other room and brought back the one book in their house.

"Are you able to read it?" Rich asked.

The boy's face lit up. "I love to read the gospel of John because it says Jesus loves children."

Indeed, as the song goes, Jesus loves "all the children of the world." There has never been anybody like Jesus to bring good news to a 13-year-old boy in a thatched hut with a pile of stones where a mom and a dad ought to be.

Stearns left his job and his house and his title and asked God for one more hill.

The logo of World Vision has its name with a little field of color and a shining star next to it. The star makes me think of the apostle Paul's call to people to "shine like stars" in an often-dark world. World Vision is only a little part of a bigger vision that's mentioned at the beginning of the book of John: "In the beginning was the Word, and the Word was with God, and the Word was God . . . And the Word was made flesh, and dwelt among us."

What we translate in English as *word* comes from the Greek word *logos*. It's where we get our word *logo*.

Jesus is God's logo.

It's as if God has said, "I want my symbol, my character, my representation, my will to be wrapped up in one single expression. It is Jesus. He is it."

Jesus is God's logo. If you want to know what a life can look like when lived with the Spirit flowing from the belly, look at Jesus. On a mountain called Calvary, on a splintered cross, the sin that needed to be cleansed, the price that needed to be paid, was finally and fully paid by Jesus.

Christians don't have a program, plan, or product to help the world. We have a Savior. We don't point to success, knowledge, pleasure, or power. We point to a cross.

What's *your* logo?

Earlier in these pages I told you a little bit about Evelyn Brand. I'll finish the story now.

This once-young girl became a little old lady, and everyone called her "Granny Brand." She spent her life in India, including 20 years as a widow. At age 70 she got word from her home mission office in England that they wouldn't give her another five-year assignment. They felt she was simply getting too old.

But she was also stubborn.

A party was held to celebrate her time in India, and everyone there cheered her on. "Have a good trip back home," they all said.

"I'll tell you a little secret," she announced. "I'm not going back home. I'm staying in India."

Evelyn had had a little shack built with some resources she'd smuggled in. Then she bought a pony to get around the mountains, and this woman in her 70s rode from village to village on horseback to tell people about Jesus. She did that for five years on her own. One day, at 75 years old, she fell off her pony and broke her hip. Her son, Paul Brand, a respected doctor, said to her, "Mom, you had a great run. God's used you. It's time to turn it over now. You go on back home."

"I am not going back home," she said.

God, give me the mountain!

Brand spent *another 18 years* traveling from village to village on horseback. Falls, concussions, sicknesses, and aging couldn't stop her. Finally, when she hit 93 years old, she couldn't ride horseback any more. So the men in these villages—because they loved Granny Brand so much—put her on a stretcher and carried her from one village to another. She lived two more years and gave those years as a gift, carried on a stretcher, to help the poorest of the poor. She died, but she never retired. She just graduated into the next life.

If Granny Brand had a logo, it wouldn't point toward success, smarts, pleasure, or power. It would be the stretcher on which she was carried up and down the mountains to pour out the end of her life in sacrificial love.

What a remarkable logo.

• • •

Your deepest craving should be to be alive with God, to become the person God made you to be, and to be used to help God's world flourish.

That's the life available to you every moment. It's the life found in Jesus, the man on the cross who mastered sin in his death and mastered death in a tomb and who now gives life with supreme authority. It's available to you in this very moment, no matter what your situation. God is at work in this hour, and God's purpose is to shape you to be not only his servant, but also his friend. Out of your belly shall flow rivers of living water. Blessed are you.

Ask for a mountain.

sources

Chapter 1: Learn Why God Made You

12: "For we are God's handiwork": Ephesians 2:10.

14: "Know that the LORD Himself": Psalm 100:3 NASB.

14: "If anyone is in Christ": 2 Corinthians 5:17.

Chapter 2: The Me I Don't Want to Be

18: Henri Nouwen, *Can You Drink the Cup?* Notre Dame, IN: Ave Maria Press, 1996, 89.

23: "We know that in all things": Romans 8:28.

23: "Rule-keeping does not": Galatians 3:12 *The Message.*

23: "I have come that you": John 10:10 paraphrased.

24: Gordon MacKenzie, *Orbiting the Giant Hairball: A Corporate Fool's Guide to Surviving with Grace.* New York: Viking, 1998, 19.

24: "With God, all things are possible": Mark 10:27 paraphrased.

25: "I have come that they": John 10:10.

25: Irenaeus, *Adversus Haereses.*

26: "Today you will be with me": Luke 23:43.

Chapter 3: Discover the Flow

30: "Let anyone who is thirsty": John 7:37–39.

31: "You will receive power": Acts 1:8.

31: "Though you have not seen [Jesus]": 1 Peter 1:8.

31: "Take my yoke upon you": Matthew 11:29.

34: "Breath of life": Genesis 2:7.

35: "Do not quench the Spirit": 1 Thessalonians 5:19 NASB.

Chapter 4: Find Out How You Grow

38: "Head and shoulders": 1 Samuel 9:2 NRSV.

38: "Tried walking around": 1 Samuel 17:39.

38: "I cannot go in these": 1 Samuel 17:39.

39: "Go, and the LORD be with you": 1 Samuel 17:37.

39: "Put on the full armor of God": Ephesians 6:11.

39: "Where the Spirit of the Lord is": 2 Corinthians 3:17.

41: "Father, may they be one with you": John 17:21 paraphrased.

Chapter 5: Surrender: The One Decision That Always Helps

46: "The fool has said in his heart, 'There is no God'": Psalm 14:1; 53:1 NASB.

46: "Be like God": Genesis 3:5.

46: "Out of our bellies can flow": John 7:38 paraphrased.

50: Roy Baumeister: M. T. Gailliot, N. L. Mead, and R. F. Baumeister, "Self-Regulation." In *Handbook of Personality, Theory and Research*, 3rd edition. Edited by O. P. John et al. New York: Guilford Press, 2008, 472–91.

52: "Let this cup pass from me": Matthew 26:39 KJV.

Chapter 6: Let Your Desires Lead You to God

56: "So Jacob served seven years": Genesis 29:20.
56: Who found a treasure: Matthew 13:44.
56: Jonathan Haidt, *The Happiness Hypothesis: Finding Modern Truth in Ancient Wisdom*. New York: Basic Books, 2005.
58: "Taste and see that the LORD": Psalm 34:8.
58: "You open your hand": Psalm 145:16–19 NIV.
58: "Whoever wants to be my disciple": Mark 8:34.
59: "Every good and perfect gift": James 1:1
60: "I have fought the good fight": 2 Timothy 4:7.
60: Jonathan and David: 1 Samuel 20.
62: "Like a gold ring in a pig's snout": Proverbs 11:22 *The Message*.

Chapter 7: Think Great Thoughts

65: "Search me, God": Psalm 139:23.
65: "The mind controlled": Romans 8:6.
66: Kept in perfect peace: See Isaiah 26:3 KJV.
66: Jeffrey Schwartz and Sharon Begley, *The Mind and the Brain: Neuroplasticity and the Power of Mental Force*. New York: Harper Perennial, 2003, 325.
71: "To what can I compare": Matthew 11:16–17 NIV.

Chapter 8: Feed Your Mind Great Stuff

73: "Blessed are those": Psalm 1:1–3.
75: "Whatever is true": Philippians 4:8.
76: "The LORD is my shepherd": Psalm 23:1 KJV.
79: "Be doers of the word": James 1:22 NRSV.
80: "Love one another": John 13:34.

Chapter 9: Never Worry Alone

82: "Peace, be still": Mark 4:39 KJV.
83: "For the Spirit God gave us": 2 Timothy 1:7.
84: "A Test to Worry About": Edward M. Hallowell, *Worry: Hope and Help for a Common Condition*. New York: Ballantine Books, 1998, 79–83.
85: "There is no fear in love": 1 John 4:18 NASB.
85: "Never worry alone.": Hallowell, *Worry: Hope and Help for a Common Condition*, xxiii.
86: "Is anyone afraid or fainthearted?": Deuteronomy 20:8.
87: "Which exceeds anything": Philippians 4:7 NLT.
88: "Out of your bellies will flow": John 7:38 paraphrased.
90: "For the Spirit God gave us": 2 Timothy 1:7.

Chapter 10: Let Your Talking Flow into Praying

95: "Where can I go from your Spirit?": Psalm 139:7–8.
96: "Looking up to pray": John 11:41 paraphrased.
96: "Father, I thank you that you have heard me": John 11:41–42.
97: "Get out of here, baldy!": 2 Kings 2:23–24.
98: Shel Silverstein, *A Light in the Attic*. New York: HarperCollins, 1981.

Chapter 11: Temptation: How *Not* to Get Hooked

100: "No temptation has overtaken you": 1 Corinthians 10:13.
100: Joseph and Potiphar's wife: Genesis 39.
101: "Do not quench the Spirit": 1 Thessalonians 5:19 NASB.
101: "I made a covenant with my eyes": Job 31:1 NIV.
102: "The joy of the LORD is your strength": Nehemiah 8:10.
102: "Rejoice in the Lord always": Philippians 4:4 NASB.
102: Sermon on the Mount: Matthew 5–7.
103: "Deliver us from evil": Matthew 6:13 KJV, NASB.

Chapter 12: Know Your Primary Flow-Blocker

105: *USA Today*: From a series of articles published in February 2003. http://www.usatoday.com/sports/ten-hardest-splash.htm.
107: Cornelius Plantinga, *Not The Way It's Supposed to Be: A Breviary of Sin*. Grand Rapids: Eerdmans, 1995, ix.
107: Michael Mangis, *Signature Sins: Taming Our Wayward Hearts*. Downers Grove, IL: InterVarsity Press, 2008.
108: Richard Rohr and Andreas Ebert, *The Enneagram: A Christian Perspective*. New York: Crossroad, 2001.
109: "Must increase": John 3:30 KJV.
111: "How good and pleasant it is": Psalm 133:1.
114: Jesus warned about people: Luke 6:41–42.

Chapter 13: When You're Out of the Flow, Jump Back In

116: Carol Tavris and Elliot Aronson, *Mistakes Were Made (But Not by Me): Why We Justify Foolish Beliefs, Bad Decisions, and Hurtful Acts*. Wilmington, MA: Houghton Mifflin/Mariner, 2008.
117: David Marcum and Steven Smith, *Egonomics: What Makes Ego Our Greatest Asset (or Most Expensive Liability)*. New York: Simon & Schuster/Fireside, 2008, 41.
118: "Who can discern their own errors?": Psalm 19:12.
120: "He did not know that the LORD": Judges 16:20.
120: The psalmist asks God to do a kind of fearless searching: See Psalm 139:23–24.
120: "Evil good and good evil": Isaiah 5:20.
120: "putting off" anger ... "putting on" those characteristics that flow from the life of the Spirit: See Ephesians 4:22–32.
125: "Brothers and sisters, if someone is caught in a sin": Galatians 6:1.
125: Frank Laubach: Cited by Dallas Willard in personal communication.

Chapter 14: Try Going Off the Deep End with God

130: "When you pray, go into your room": Matthew 6:6.
130: "As he was praying, the heavens opened": Luke 3:21–22 TLB.
130: "The news about him spread": Luke 5:15–16.
130: "One of those days Jesus went out": Luke 6:12–13.
131: "When Jesus heard what had happened": Matthew 14:13.
131: "While it was still dark, Jesus got up": Mark 1:35, 38.
131: "Satan has asked to sift all of you": Luke 22:31–32.

131: "Jesus went out as usual": Luke 22:39–42.
131: "As he was praying": Luke 9:29.
131: "God's Spirit is right alongside": Romans 8:26–27 *The Message*.
134: "The LORD bless you": Numbers 6:24–26 NRSV.

Chapter 15: Make Sure Your Relationships Are Life-Giving

136: "The fellowship of the Spirit": See, for example, 2 Corinthians 6:14; 13:14; Philippians 2:1; 1 John 1:6.
137: "It isn't good for man": Genesis 2:18 TLB.
137: "Being rooted and established": Ephesians 3:17.
137: Donald Winnicott, *The Maturational Processes and the Facilitating Environment*. London: Hogarth Press, 1960.
140: "Anyone who does not love": 1 John 3:14.
140: "You, my brothers and sisters": Galatians 5:13.
141: "Let us consider how we may": Hebrew 10:24–25.
141: Robert Putnam, *Bowling Alone: The Collapse and Revival of American Community*. New York: Simon & Schuster, 2000, 332.

Chapter 16: Be Human

147: "A man after [God's] own heart": 1 Samuel 13:14.
149: "With glad and sincere hearts": Acts 2:46.
149: "Accept one another, then": Romans 15:7.
150: "Confess your sins to one another": James 5:16 NASB.
151: Do you remember when: See Matthew 14:28–31; John 18:10; John 13:36–38 and 18:15–18; Matthew 16:22–23

Chapter 17: Find a Few Difficult People to Help You Grow

153: George Bernard Shaw: Source unknown.
154: "You're familiar with the old written law": Matthew 5:43–48 *The Message*.
155: Jill Bolte Taylor, *My Stroke of Insight: A Brain Scientist's Personal Journey*. New York: Viking, 2008, 74.
157: "Do not grieve the Holy Spirit": Ephesians 4:30–31.
157: "Life-giving quarter-second": Daniel Goleman, *Emotional Intelligence: Why It Can Matter More Than IQ*. New York: Bantam Books, 1995.
157: "In your anger do not sin": Ephesians 4:26–27.
158: "If anyone forces you to go one mile": Matthew 5:41.
159: Charles Lamb: Source unknown.

Chapter 18: You've Gotta Go through Some Junk before You Come Back Home

164: Haidt, *The Happiness Hypothesis*.
164: Robert C. Roberts, *Spiritual Emotions: A Psychology of Christian Virtues*. Grand Rapids: Eerdmans, 2007, 148ff.
167: Ernest Hemingway: Source unknown.
169: "The LORD was with Joseph": Genesis 39:2.
169: "We know that in all things": Romans 8:28.
169: "God ... will not let you be tempted beyond what you can bear": See 1 Corinthians 10:13.

170: They could command a mountain: See Mark 11:23.

171: "Mourn with those who mourn": Romans 12:15.

172: Joni Eareckson Tada: See, for example, *Joni: An Unforgettable Story* (Grand Rapids: Zondervan, 1976) and *A Lifetime of Wisdom: Embracing the Way God Heals You* (Grand Rapids: Zondervan, 2009).

172: Bill Dallas, *Lessons from San Quentin: Everything I Needed to Know about Life I Learned in Prison*. Wheaton, IL: Tyndale, 2009.

174: All creation is groaning for redemption: See Romans 8:22.

Chapter 19: Ask for a Mountain

178: "Whoever wants to be my disciple": Matthew 16:24; Mark 8:34; Luke 9:23.

180: When the spies returned: See Numbers 14:3–4.

180: "We can certainly do it": Numbers 13:30.

180: "I was forty years old when Moses": Joshua 14:7–8.

181: Martin Seligman, *Authentic Happiness: Using the New Positive Psychology to Realize Your Potential for Lasting Fulfillment*. New York: Simon & Schuster/Free Press, 2002, 4.

181: "Faith-filled people": Seligman, *Authentic Happiness*, 40ff.

181: Granny Brand: Paul W. Brand and Philip Yancey, *Fearfully and Wonderfully Made*. Grand Rapids: Zondervan, 1980.

182: "So here I am today, eighty-five years old!": Joshua 14:10–12.

182: "We saw the descendants of Anakites there": Numbers 13:33 paraphrased.

183: Joshua became the new leader: See Deuteronomy 34:9; Joshua 1:1–3.

183: Marian Diamond, "Optimism about the Aging Brain," *Aging Today*, May-June 1998. See http://www.asaging.org/at/at-193/diamond.html (accessed 21 September 2009).

184: Rich Stearns, *The Hole in Our Gospel: What Does God Expect of Us? The Answer That Changed My Life and Might Just Change the World*. Nashville: Thomas Nelson, 2009.

185: "All the children of the world": From "Jesus Loves the Little Children." Words by C. Herbert Woolston; tune by George F. Root.

185: "Shine like stars": Philippians 2:15 NIV.

186: "In the beginning was the Word": John 1:1, 14 KJV.